Zen of LaunchPad

Version 4.3

Dr. Chen-Hanson Ting

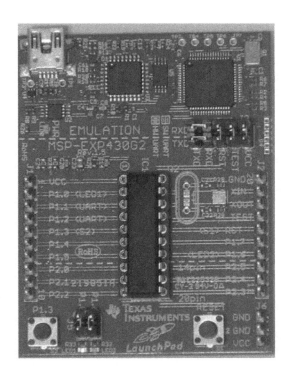

Offete Enterprises, Inc. 2015

This Book is Copyright © ExMark, 02 October 2018

The current Forth Bookshelf can be found at
https://www.amazon.co.uk/Juergen-Pintaske/e/B00N8HVEZM

All 20 available as eBook. The P after the number notes available as print book as well

Contents

Link to IDE and code image for download:

http://wiki.forth-ev.de/doku.php/en:projects:430eforth:start

More information and option Naken Assembler on github:

https://github.com/mikalus/eForth43-msp430g2553-naken

Version: 2016_10_24v10_2018_10_27v1 _print, 27 October 2018, ExMark

Chapter 1. Zen of Things

Zen is the most popular branch of Buddhism in China and Japan. It was introduced by Bodhidharma (~535AD) in the late fifth century to China. For hundreds of years, the Zen teaching was passed from masters to masters as an oral tradition. Only the Sixth Patriarch Huineng in Tang Dynasty (638-713AD) had his lectures recorded to become the Platform Sutra, capturing the essence of Zen on paper. Even then, Zen is elusive, and open to all kinds of interpretations and practices.

The meaning of Zen is meditation. Why meditate? To achieve enlightenment. What is enlightenment? Nobody really knows, and nobody can tell. The best story about Zen and enlightenment was that one day Śākyamuni Buddha (~500BC), the original enlightened one, lifted a flower to show his disciples. Nobody knew what he meant. Only Mahākāśyapa smiled and Buddha announced that Mahākāśyapa got enlightened. So the story was told that the enlightenment passed on from Mahākāśyapa through 28 generations of masters, until Bodhidharma brought it to China.

1.1 Forth, Zen of Computer

Forth was invented by Chuck Moore in the 1960s as a programming language. Chuck was not impressed by programming languages, operating systems, and computer hardware of that time. He sought the simplest and most efficient way to control his computers. He used Forth to program every computer in his sight. And then, he found that he could design better computers in transistors and gates, because Forth is much more than just a programming language; it is also an excellent computer architecture.

Many books and many papers had been written about Forth. However, Forth is still elusive, because it has many features and characteristics which are difficult to describe. Now that it has moved from software to hardware, with technologies like FPGA and custom VLSI, it is even more difficult to accurately put it into words. Here I will try to look at it from a completely different angle.

Forth is a list processor. It is very similar to LISP in spirit, but totally different in form. Both languages assume that all computable problems can be expressed and solved in nested lists. LISP is a top-down list processor. From the top, it has to look forward to sub lists yet to be defined. All it can do is to name the sub lists, and delineate their structures in parentheses. The sub lists will be substantiated or resolved later.

Forth is a bottom-up list processor. Subsists must be built before they can be nested into lists at a higher level. No forward reference is allowed. No parenthesis is necessary. Deeply nested lists are built from inside out. Subsists can be, and must be, tested and debugged exhaustively, before using them to build the next layer of lists. Practically, this bottom up approach results in more reliable programs, running faster, using less memory, and costing less in shorter development time.

Forth is a LISP without the irritating superfluous parentheses.

Forth has a set of commands, and a set of interpreters to interpret lists of commands.

Forth commands are records stored in memory. They are generally linked into a searchable chain called a dictionary. Forth language is very similar to the English language. Forth commands are often called words. Like English, words are usually defined by many other words. Like English, words and their definitions are collected in a searchable dictionary.

A record of a Forth command has three fields: a link field linking all commands to form a searchable dictionary, a name field containing the name of this command as an ASCII string which can be searched, and a code field containing executable code and data to perform a specific function for this command. It may have an optional parameter field, which contains additional data needed by this command. The link field and name field allow a text interpreter to look up a command in the dictionary, and the code field provides executable code to perform the function assigned for this command.

Forth commands have two representations: an external representation in the form of text strings with ASCII characters for human consumption; and an internal representation in the form of a token, which invokes executable code to be executed by a computer. In many Forth systems, the tokens are addresses. However, tokens can take many other forms depending on implementation. For example, Java, which is a variant of Forth, uses byte tokens.

There are two types of Forth commands: primitive Forth commands having machine code in their code fields, and compound Forth commands having token lists in their code fields.

A Forth Virtual Machine is a computer which can interpret--process or execute-- Forth commands. Forth uses two types of interpreters: a text interpreter or outer interpreter which process Forth commands in the external or text representation, and a set of inner interpreters which process Forth commands in the internal representations of tokens.

The text interpreter processes lists of commands into text strings. A list of Forth commands contains a sequence of strings representing Forth commands, separated by white spaces and terminated by a carriage return:

```
<list of command strings>  <enter>
```

The text interpreter parses out commands in the text strings, coverts strings into tokens, and the inner interpreter executes code represented by these tokens. Each command has an embedded inner interpreter which executes or interprets this command. The inner interpreter of a primitive command simply executes the machine code in its code field. The inner interpreter of a compound command processes the token list in its code field. How it processes the token list depends upon how tokens are defined and implemented.

The text interpreter operates in two modes: interpreting mode and compiling mode. In the interpreting mode, a list of command names is interpreted; i.e., command strings are parsed and executed. In the compiling mode, a list of command strings is compiled; i.e., commands are parsed and corresponding tokens are compiled into a token list. This token list is given a name to form a new compound command, adding a new command record in the dictionary.

New compound commands are compiled to represent token lists. This is the most powerful feature of Forth, in that you can compile new compound commands, which replace lists of existing commands, both primitive and compound. The syntax to compile a new compound command is:

```
:   <name>   <list of existing commands>   ;
```

Nested token lists are added as new compound commands until the final compound command becomes the solution of your application. Lists are compiled and tested from the bottom up. The solution space can be explored wider and farther, and an optimized solution can be found more quickly. Program correctness can be proven in this bottom-up list building process.

Linear, sequential token lists are enhanced by control structures like branch structures and loop structures. A structure is a token list inside which the execution sequence can be modified dynamically. The following figure shows a sequential structure, a branch structure and a loop structure.

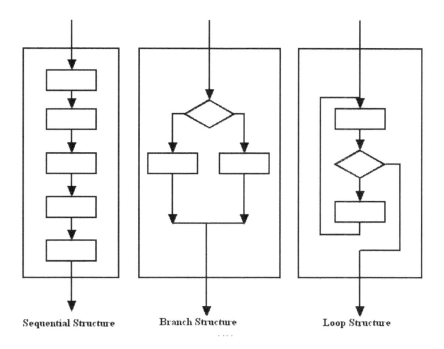

Sequential Structure   **Branch Structure**   **Loop Structure**

A structure has only one entry point and one exit point, although it may have many branches inside. Structures can be nested, but may not overlap with one another. A structure can therefore be considered an enhanced token. A compound command is then a structure given a name.

Using the concept of structures, a new compound command has the following syntax:

```
:   <name>   <list of structures>   ;
```

The inner interpreter executes tokens in nested token lists. When a token represents a primitive command, the primitive command inner interpreter executes the machine instructions in the code. A primitive command must be terminated by a machine instruction, or a short machine instruction sequence, $NEXT, which returns to execute the next token in the token list being processed.

When a token represents a compound command, the first commands in the token list must be a machine instruction, or a short instructions sequence, $NEST, which pushes the address of the next token in the previous list on a return stack, and then starts to process the token list in the present compound command. The present token list must be terminated by a command, or a machine instruction sequence, $EXIT, which pops the address saved on the return stack, and continue process the previous token list which called the present compound command.

$NEXT, $NEST and $EXIT are the inner interpreters. An inner interpreter is not a centralized mechanism to execute Forth commands. Inner interpreters are dispersed in all Forth commands, which automatically invoke the next command to execute after completing their own tasks. They allow tokens in deeply nested token lists to be processed automatically and efficiently.

The fundamental reason why Forth lists (command lists or token lists) can be simple, linear sequences of commands is that Forth uses two stacks: a return stack to store nested return addresses, and a parameter stack to pass parameters among nested commands. Parameters are passed implicitly on the parameter stack, and do not have to be explicitly invoked. Therefore, Forth commands can be interpreted in a linear sequence, and tokens can be stored in simple, linear token lists. Language syntax is greatly simplified, internal representation of code is greatly simplified, and execution speed is greatly increased.

A Forth Virtual Machine is a computer architecture, which supports the text and inner interpreters, and a set of commands in a command dictionary. It thus needs two stacks, efficient means to traverse nested token lists, and a virtual CPU with a small set of primitive commands, and an extensible while unlimited set of compound commands.

It is an interesting point of view to look at Forth as a list processor. I have not seen a formal proof that lists can solve all computable problems. But, I have yet to encounter a problem which cannot be solved by Forth as nested lists. In practice, the solution to any problem in the form of nested lists generally is the most compact and most efficient.

Returning to the English language analogue, Forth language is a collection of commands, or words. Most Forth words replace lists of existing words, and new words are added freely. It mimics a natural language even simpler than English, more like Chinese, without complicated and artificial syntax rules. It mimics how we humans think, reason, and communicate, in the simplest fashion. It is natural intelligence, much superior to any scheme conceived as artificial intelligence. It is also the simplest way we can impart our intelligence into computers, microcontrollers, and other intelligent machines.

Hence, I declare: Forth is Zen of Computer.

Existing documentation on most Forth systems consisted of mainly an alphabetically sorted glossary, like an English dictionary. However, knowledge is never a glossary, which contains fragmented information not connected to each other. I was very happy to see that in 1974 the great Encyclopedia Britannica split into a Micropedia, a Macropedia, and a Propedia which contained outlines of every branch of knowledge. That's how knowledge should be organized and presented.

In this book, I try to present a complete Forth system according to the loading order: first the small pieces of elementary commands forming the Forth Virtual Machine, and then these commands are used to build more complicated and more powerful compound commands performing special tasks required by the text interpreter, and then the text interpreter itself. After that, command compiler and other tools are added to complete the system. Knowledge builds up gradually and you are led to think at higher and higher abstract levels.

At the highest abstract level, Forth is actually a list processor. It shares with LISP the basic assumption that all computable problems can be solved by nested lists. Facing a simple minded human user, the text interpreter interprets short lists of commands typed in from a terminal as a list of character strings. Driving a fast and complicated computer, the inner interpreters in Forth Virtual Machine process deeply nested lists of tokens to translate deeply convoluted ideas expressed in layers upon layers of compound commands to actions demanded by your thinking at very high abstract levels.

It is incredible that a simple command compiler which turns a simple list of command strings into a token list, giving it a name to form a new compound command, has the unlimited power to solve problems of any complexity. But, this is what Forth is. This is what Zen is about.

The most interesting aspect of Forth is that it retains names of commands in memory. Most other programming languages throw away the names after code is compiled. Names were only temporary devices used for the convenience of the programmer in the process of programming, and they are of no value in the final product. In a living and growing computing system, just like in natural languages, names are representations of intelligence and are the only vehicles for thinking, reasoning, abstraction, communication, and accumulation of knowledge and technology. Lao - Tze was the first person who realized the significance of names along with Tao.

He had profound understanding of nature, and perhaps, computers. He opened his Tao-Te Ching with some profound statements. Nobody really knows what he's talking about, but I do, because I think he was talking about computers. I will show you my translation and my interpretation. The Chinese text was based on a recently (1973) excavated version of Tao-Te Ching, similar to but not the same as you find in your local library.

道可道也，非恆道也。	Eternal Tao cannot be spoken,
名可名也，非恆名也。	Eternal name cannot be named.
無名萬物之始也；	In the beginning, Tao has no name,
有名萬物之母也。	But, Name is the mother of everything.
故恆無欲也，以觀其眇；	Tao is manifested by its actions,
恆有欲也，以觀其所噭。	Name reveals the nature of Tao.
兩者同出，異名同胃，	Tao and Name are one and same,
玄之有玄，眾眇之門。	Uttermost profound, mystery of mysteries!

Lao-Tze was talking about Tao and Name. Tao as Nature, can be observed. To understand Tao, and to communicate Tao, we need Names. I think he was actually talking about computers and firmware engineering. A computer has two components. It has programs which can do wonderful things beyond human comprehension. Programs are best modularized and constructed in nested lists. If all modules and lists are given proper names, programs can be constructed, debugged, understood, and used most efficiently by human.

It is then very obvious in Forth, Tao is the executable code in the code field of a command, and Name is the name in the name field. Tao does things, and Name entails relationship, knowledge, understanding, and abstraction. Human intelligence is based on names, or words. Words are built on other words. We think with words. We communicate with words. We express deeply convoluted ideas with words. Modern sciences and engineering use many other symbols and drawing when words are not sufficient, but computer sciences and firmware engineering use plain words.

Software engineers and firmware engineers throw away the words they used to build target systems, because these words are not needed by the end users, who are generally assumed to be monkeys who can only push keys and click mouse. Users do not need knowledge on how the product was constructed. However, if you are a user of your program, you want to keep the names as long as you are using it. You might have to go back to some words to find bugs if the program had trouble. Were the words properly preserved in the product, you would have a much easier time to find bugs and fix them.

This is what Forth is. Names are preserved with Tao. Replacing a list of names with a new name is how natural languages were developed, how they are used, and how they are evolving. Forth is therefore natural intelligence, not merely artificial intelligence. You think in this way. Why not program in the same way? You want to keep the names in your system as long as you have ownership. You can always strip the names out later, if you are concerned about your intellectual properties.

道與名.　　Tao and Name. Commands with names. That's Forth. Zen of computer.

1.2 LaunchPad, Zen of Microcontroller

All these years, I have been looking for microcontroller platforms on which I can teach people how to program in Forth language. I designed a training course called *Firmware Engineering Workshop*, originally for an 8051 microcontroller kit. With it, I could train an open minded engineer to program in Forth in about a week. The kit was a reasonable capable platform, i.e., an 8051 microcontroller evaluation board with a Forth operating system loaded. In the old days, good platforms were expensive, and low cost platforms were inadequate. What I did was to grab any microcontroller board at hand and used it. It did not work well because what I taught could not be easily replicated by people at home. People got frustrated when they could not reproduce results I demonstrated. Then, TI gave us the LaunchPad Kit.

The microcontroller evaluation board I need must have a microcontroller with reasonable capabilities. An 8-bit microcontroller with a fast clock is adequate. 16-bit or 32-bit microcontrollers are of course much better. The board must have at least 8 KB of ROM memory and 1 KB of RAM memory. The more RAM the better. It must also have a USART port to communicate with a terminal emulator on a host PC. Any other I/O devices will be icings on the cake. The more the better.

In June 2010, TI released MSP430 LaunchPad Kit. Selling at $4.30, it was a joke. The price was less than the postage to ship it. But, what's to lose? I bought two, just to see if it was real. It was. LaunchPad was an interesting little board, with a 20 pin DIP socket. However, the chip installed in the socket at the time, MSP430G2231, had only 14 pins. It had only 2 KB of flash memory and did not seem to be useful for any substantial application. The kits were shelved and forgotten.

In late 2011, a Taiwan FIG member, Luke Chang, announced a tinyForth for LaunchPad Kit. Luke was a legend in Taiwan. He is an electrical engineer in the Center of Precision Instruments, which is an organization under the National Science Council, chartered to develop scientific instruments and their maintenance for universities and research institutes.

His fame was that he could revive any dead instrument, no matter how complicated or sophisticated it was. He generally removed the CPU chip in an instrument, connected bus signals to an 8051 board, and debugged the instrument using his 8051 Forth system. He also developed a universal assembler based on Win32Forth and TCOM, which he used to build Forth systems for many CPUs. He usually was the first person to get Forth running on any new CPU.

tinyForth was tiny, but the target compiler in Win32Forth was not. It was difficult to trace Luke's thoughts in his target compiler. Then I thought that I could squeeze a simple and small Forth system into the 2 KB flash of LaunchPad. Normally, an eForth system needed about 6 KB of memory. It was interesting to see what could be done with 2 KB. This eForth implementation was called 430uForth, for 430 Micro Forth. I retained only the text interpreter, and a minimal number of commands to support the interpreter. I talked about it in the Silicon Valley Forth Interest Group (SVFIG), but never published it. It was only for my personal enjoyment and edification.

Then in May 2012, Kevin Appert in SVFIG told me that he got a newer LaunchPad Kit with MSP430G2553, which had 16 KB of flash memory. He loaned it to me so I could port the complete eForth model over. It was 430eForth v1.0. I posted it on my website www.offete.com. It was listed there with 328eForth for Arduino Uno Kit and Stm8eForth for the STM8S-Discovery Kit from STMicroelectronics. Only 328eForth generated traffic. There were very little interests in 430eForth and Stm8eForth. I was occupied by other projects and returned the kit to Kevin.

A couple of months ago, in June 2014, I was introduction by Juergen Pintaske to Dirk Bruehl and Michael Kalus, and to the 4E4th project, Forth for Education on LaunchPad. It was a group project of Forth-Gesellschaft, eV in Lower Rhine, Germany, porting

CamelForth430 by Brad Rodriquez to MSP430 LaunchPad. It was bundled with a nice 4E4th-IDE so that young students could get Forth up on a LaunchPad quickly and do experiments on it. Dirk Bruehl even made me a package 430eForth-IDE to boot 430eForth up without using TI's complicated Code Composer Studio toolchains.

I dug up my LaunchPad collection, and found two old LaunchPad Kits, in version 1.4, and 4 MSP430G2553 chips. I was quite sure that they had 430eForth on them, but none of the kits worked. I started to panic. Forth normally does not die on itself. Evidently, the boards and the chips had aged. I still had the old Dell XP computer on which 430eForth was implemented, but now I am using an HP Windows 7 computer. I copied everything from Dell to HP, but nothing worked.

After I re-learnt the newer Code Composer Studio 6, 430eForth started to work intermittently, and then consistently on one of my LaunchPad Kits. The other LaunchPad Kit just refused to download 430eForth object file, no matter what. But, Dirk assured me that 430eForth was OK, because he had brought it up, after he installed Code Composer Studio. That was a big relief. I thought of retracting 430eForth from my website.

I had a software USART in 430eForth, because the internal clock in MSP430G2553 was about 1.1 MHz, and the data sheet said it was not accurate enough for timing purposes. I assumed that I could not depend upon it to run the USART port, and implemented a software USART. The downside of it was that I could not raise the baud rate above 2400 baud. It slowed down eForth considerably, especially when I sent text files from HyperTerminal to LaunchPad. It was barely tolerable.

CamelForth, however, runs at 9600 baud. Dirk enlightened me that TI actually calibrated the internal clock in every MSP430G2 chip so that it could run accurately at 1, 8, 12 and 16 MHz. I didn't read the data sheet thoroughly enough to learn this feature. This internal clock was called DCOCLK, a digitally controlled oscillator. TI stored the calibration constants in the Information Flash Memory Segment A, from $10F8 to $10FF. Dirk sent me code from CamelForth which initialized the DCO to run USART at 9600 baud.

I modified my code accordingly, but no luck. LaunchPad just would not talk. Only at this time, I wished I had an oscilloscope. All these years, I was kind of proud of myself, building all the embedded systems without an oscilloscope, or a logic analyzer. Not knowing what the USART was doing, was killing me. After spending a couple of days wondering and trying things, it occurred to me that I better check the Information Memory Segment A. For sure, in three of my 4 MSP430G2553 chips, the Information

Memory A was erased. Even with the chip which retained the calibration constants, 430eForth still did not work. I had abused these chips and kits so much, that they decided to revolt together.

I told Dirk about the calibration constants, and sent him my modified 430eForth assembly file. He tested the code and told me that it worked on his LaunchPad. He was very generous in sending me 7 fresh 2553 chips in a two-day priority box. I waited earnestly for the box to arrive. Plug in a fresh 2553 chip, and Ureka! 430eForth ran at 9600 baud.

MSP430G2 LaunchPad is essentially *the* single chip microcontroller MSP430G2553. The emulation part of LaunchPad, which provides an USB interface to a host PC, is much more complicated than the microcontroller itself. The USB interface contains an USART device and a Spy-Bi-Wire-Test programming and debugging device. Fortunately, I did not have to understand this part of LaunchPad. Its complication is hidden behind the USB interface chip, MSP430F1612IPMR, and the USB driver on PC. Once the USB driver is installed on PC, and LaunchPad is connected to PC through an USB cable, MSP430G2553 can be programmed and debugged transparently from 430eForth-IDE.

The PC industry painted itself into a tight corner of USB, and got rid of the simple USART COM ports and the parallel printer PRT port. For microcontroller programming and communications, a simple USART port is all that I need. The upside of this trend is that PC has replaced all the expensive hardware IDE tools necessary for microcontroller programming and firmware engineering.

Assuming that the USB interface allows easy and transparent access to the microcontroller, the hardware we need to develop microcontroller applications is reduced to a small printed circuit board like LaunchPad and an USB cable, besides a PC which is universally available on every desktop. As TI emphasizes in the *LaunchPad User's Guide*, LaunchPad is a platform that allows us to develop microcontroller applications for many MSP430 chips, as well as other interesting systems like its popular eZ430-Chronos Watch Module.

Hardware tools for firmware engineering have been reduced to the absolute minimum, a small printed circuit board with a target microcontroller. LaunchPad is very close to my ideal firmware engineering platform. It is Zen of microcontroller.

1.3 430eForth, Zen of Forth

I thought I attained enlightenment after I wrote my first Forth system on a Nova 4 minicomputer from Data General. At the time, I had just learnt polyForth from Forth, Inc, on a PDP-11 minicomputer. I could write Forth code to control an image processor, but had no idea how it worked. Chuck Moore was very certain that nobody could understand his code, and Forth, Inc. generously gave away the complete source code with each polyForth implementation.

The source code was extraterrestrial. In blocks! The Forth system was built by a metacompiler, and you didn't have a clue where it started. Then I joint Forth Interest Group (FIG), and read the PDP-11 figForth by John James. It was still mystic, but at least the assembly source code was humanly readable. Bill Ragsdale had reverse-engineered a Forth system on Apple II, and organized a Forth implementation team to port it to 6 different microcomputers.

In one of the FIG meetings, I got a copy of Nova Forth document from UC San Diego. The source code was apparently written by Chuck Moore, based on a target compiler. Immersing myself in the source code of polyForth, Nova Forth, PDP-11 figForth, and the *figForth Implementation Guide*, I managed to write a figForth for Nova 4. That was enlightenment. That was the complete understanding of a computer, and of an operating system. The computer talked to me! That was Zen. I dumped my understanding and excitement into my first Forth book: *Systems Guide to figForth*, which was enthusiastically approved by FIG members.

At the time, FIG had two standing jokes: that Forth was a Write-Only Language (WOL, as compared to Read-Only-Memory ROM), and that Forth programmers all ate Chinese food with chopsticks. The first joke was on that even Forth programmers could not read their own code. The second joke was that Bill Ragsdale fed his Forth Implementation Team with take-out food from a nearby Chinese restaurant, so everybody had to use chopsticks. Now, here came this native chopstick wading warrior laid the mythical dragon of Write-Only Language to rest.

At that time of late 70's, FIG really did not know where the microcomputer industry was heading, and Forth Implementation Team fired shots in the dark, hoping to hit a bird. It published 6 implementations for 1802, 6502, 6800, 8080, PDP11, and Alpha Micro. These implementations caught the fancy of many programmers, who contributed implementations for many other microprocessors.

After 5 years of confusion, in the early 80's, things got a little bit clearer. Intel was a go. Motorola was a go. MSDOS was a go. CPM was a go. Apple was a maybe. Henry Laxen and Mike Perry released the F83 Model. They still didn't know which processors or operating system would prevail, and built F83 Model on 8086 for MSDOS and CPM, and 8051and 68000 for CPM. In 1988, it became clear that Microsoft and Intel would dominate, and Tom Zimmer built his FPC, a Forth solely for MSDOS on IBM-PC.

In 1990, people in FIG milled around and speculated what the computers would become in the 21st century, and what kind of Forth systems would serve the needs of the new generations of Forth programmers. 3 branches of thoughts evolved: Chuck Moore went off to build Forth chips; Tom Zimmer and Andrew McKewan expanded FPC for Windows to become Win32Forth; Bill Muench and I built the eForth Model.

In the eForth Model, we intended to continue the tradition of the figForth Model, and to provide a small Forth model to a wide range of old and new microcontrollers. It had to be small, simple, and easy to understand, so that programmers and engineers not familiar with Forth language could still read the assembly source code, port it to microcontrollers of their choice, and use it to build substantial applications. The primary concern of the original eForth Model was portability. Bill Muench identified 31 commands which had to be written in machine instructions of a target microcontroller, and the rest of 223 commands written in high level Forth code could be ported without modifications.

My second enlightenment stroke when I compared the eForth Model and the MuP21 chip Chuck Moore built. The 31 eForth primitive commands and the 24 machine instructions in MuP21 matched remarkably, with very minor differences due to architectural necessity. A Forth Virtual Machine and a real Forth CPU must have the following small set of commands or instructions:

Transfer Instructions	JMP, JZ, JC, CALL, RET, LOOP
Math/Logic Instructions	AND, OR, XOR, NOT, SHR, ADDC
Memory Instructions	LDR, STR, LIT
Stack Instructions	PUSH, POP, DUP, DROP, SWAP, OVER, NOP

In MuP21, all these instructions were executed in a single clock cycle. The most amazing thing I learnt was that computers did not have to be complicated. With a simple CPU core, you could add more instructions, more hardware peripherals, more specialized coprocessors, etc. Anything you left out in hardware, you could amend it in software. The earth is flat! You could get there from here. The boundaries separating transistors, gates, logic, memory, CPU, peripherals, assembly language, high level language, and application all but disappeared. You could design and optimize your application in any of these areas. You are free! That's Zen, squared.

In the beginning, Chuck Moore created Forth with the Indirect Thread Model. In each command record, there were 4 fields: link field, name field, code field, and parameter field. The code field was the most interesting. It contained a pointer, pointing to a short routine which could interpret the data stored in the parameter field. For a primitive command, this pointer simply points to the parameter field, to execute the machine instructions stored in the parameter field.

For a compound command, this pointer points to a routine called DOCOLON, which interpreted the token list of execution addresses in the parameter field. Every command thus carried its own interpreter which was called an inner interpreter of the command. This mechanism was simple but extremely powerful. You could design your own inner interpreter to interpret your special command with a data structure you designed yourself.

figForth adopted the indirect thread model. A dogmatic guru in FIG even declared: "If it is not indirect threaded, it is not Forth!" As Forth people always did, each went off in his own way, and implemented many different thread models.

The original eForth Model was based on the Direct Thread Model. In late 90's, I used it extensively in all my professional employments, and optimized each implementation for the particular microcontroller used in each application. Particularly, I switched from the Direct Thread Model to Subroutine Thread Model, and re-coded as many high-level commands to machine instructions for better performance. The earlier direct thread implementations were then classified as eForth1 Models, and the later optimized subroutine thread implementations were classified as eForth2 Models.

Conceptually the Subroutine Thread Model is simpler, because the Forth inner interpreter is the CPU itself, and high-level compound commands have the same structure as the low level primitive commands. The token list in a high level compound command is just a sequence of subroutine call machine instructions. Nesting and unnesting of token lists are performed naturally as subroutine calls and subroutine returns, respectively, by the microcontroller itself.

A layer of inner interpreters was removed from the Forth Virtual Machine, making things easier to explain. Additional benefits were that tokens as subroutine calls can be freely mixed with machine instructions for improved performance, and interrupt service routines could be written conveniently as high level Forth commands, if you just replaced the RET instruction at end by a RETI instruction.

Since 2000, I was totally committed to subroutine thread model and used it for all my later eForth2 implementations. It was very successful for industrial applications which demanded performance rather than portability, with newer and more capable microcontrollers. I was fully convinced of the superiority of Subroutine Thread Model as I developed the P-Series of microcontrollers, following Chuck Moore's MuP21 design. When you had hardware parameter stack and return stack all integrated into one CPU core, subroutine call and return instructions were executed in a single clock cycle, just like all the other instructions. Subroutine Thread Model seemed to be the only way to construct Forth Virtual Machine.

The ARM chips did not support stacks. Nevertheless, it has a 1-level return stack in the form of a Link Register. The subroutine thread model worked beautifully on ARM chips, as subroutine call instructions were replaced by Branch-Link instructions, and subroutine return is a BX LR instruction. Nesting a subroutine call is a simple STMD R2!,(LR), and unnesting it is a LDMFD R2!,(PC). Oh, boy. People do build chips for Forth Virtual Machines, not actually aware what they were doing.

Dirk Bruehl helped me revive my LaunchPads, and made me a package 430eForth-IDE to boot 430eForth up without using TI's complicated Code Composer Studio. I vowed to clean up 430eForth and revised the user manual. I wanted a smallest, fastest, and easiest Forth to run on LaunchPad, and I thought of naming this manual *Zen of LaunchPad*.

In the original eForth Model, there are many features not necessary for small, embedded, microcontroller applications. They are in the following list:

- Multitasking
- Multiple threads (vocabularies) in dictionary
- Separated headers from code dictionary
- CATCH-THROW for error recovery
- File interface
- Decompiler

All commands supporting these features are eliminated. There are also many commands which are used to build the text interpreter and the command compiler, but are never used in applications. Their headers are removed and are not accessible by users. The size of the object code is thus significantly reduced. A much smaller set of commands is presented to the user, while the programming capability is not diminished. I also tried very hard to speed up the 430eForth system by converting as many compound commands to primitive commands, pushing the MSP430G2 microcontroller to its limit.

As I was earnestly optimizing my code and revising the documentation, Michael Kalus demonstrated to me that on the MSP430G2 microcontroller, indirect thread model used in 4E4th is actually faster than subroutine thread model, as well as using less memory. This CPU has an indirect auto-incrementing memory read mode, or post-incrementing read mode, which makes it very efficient to interpret a token list in a compound command.

After finishing optimizing my subroutine thread 430eForth v3.3, I decided to investigate the indirect thread model in CamelForth and the direct thread model in the original eForth Model, to make sure that I am writing about the best Forth for *Zen of LaunchPad.* I opened the original 8086eForth, and built two 430eForth systems from it, as the token lists of compound commands in indirect thread model are identical to those in direct thread model. All primitive commands were copied from the subroutine thread model with very little changes. 430eForth v4.3 was in direct thread model, and 430eForth v6.1 was in indirect thread model. I didn't want to leave no stone unturned.

The following figure summarizes the three thread models:

Link Field	Link Field	Link Field	Link Field	Link Field	Link Field
Name Field	Name Field	Name Field	Name Field	Name Field	Name Field
Code Field DOCOLON	Code Field $+2	Code Field CALL DOLST			
Parameter Field Address Token List	Parameter Field Machine Instructions	Code Field Adress Token List	Code Field Machine Instructions	Code Field Token List of Subroutine Call Instructions	Code Field Machine Instructions
EXIT	$NEXT	EXIT	$NEXT	RET	RET
Compound command	Primitive Command	Compound command	Primitive Command	Compound command	Primitive Command
Indirect Thread Model		Direct Thread Model		Subroutine Thread Model	

As you can see, the indirect thread model has a code field containing a pointer to an inner interpreter, and its parameter field contains either machine instructions or a token list. The direct and subroutine thread models have only one code field, containing executable machine instructions.

However, in direct thread model, a compound command has the first executable instructions as a CALL DOLST instruction, which interprets the following token list. On the other hand, in the subroutine thread model, the compound command has a token list of subroutine call instructions.

The inner interpreters in these three models are shown in detail here:

Macros	Indirect Thread	Direct Thread	Subroutine Thread
$NEXT	mov @ip+,w mov @w+,pc	mov @ip+,pc	ret
$NEST	DOCOLON	call #DOLST	Call <addr>
	DOCOLN: push ip mov w,ip $NEXT	DOLST: pop w push ip mov w,ip $NEXT	
$UNNEST	EXIT	EXIT	Ret
	EXIT: pop ip $NEXT	EXIT: pop ip $NEXT	
Token	Execution address	Execution address	Call <addr>

The most interesting thing is that in direct thread model, the inner interpreter $NEXT is reduced to a single MSP430G2 instruction mov @ip+,pc. So much more can be accomplished in adding just one single indirect auto-incrementing memory read mode to a fairly ordinary instruction set! This single instruction $NEXT also pushes the performance of direct thread model over the other two models, as shown in the following table:

	Indirect Thread	Direct Thread	Subroutine Thread
Overhead for primitives	6 bytes 4 cycles	4 bytes 2 cycles	6 bytes 8 cycles
Overhead for colon words	8 bytes 12 cycles	8 bytes 17 cycles	6 bytes 8 cycles
Object code	4180 bytes	4136 bytes	4890 bytes
Source code	40,453 bytes	39,453 bytes	42,323 bytes
10M empty loops	16 sec	12 sec	18 sec
10K Searches 12345	23 sec	19 sec	24 sec

The memory is reduced to 4136 bytes in the direct thread model. This is absolutely the smallest working Forth system with a text interpreter, a command compiler, and some debugging tools for any microcontroller, ever! I tried to get it down under 4KB, but no luck yet.

The empty loop test is definitely not a fair test, because it only exercises the branch back code in DONXT. Searching a number string is fairer, because it searches the entire dictionary before doing a number conversion. The results show that all three models perform almost equally well.

Nevertheless, these tests gave me an excuse to go back to my earlier book *eForth and Zen*, using the direct thread model on the LauchPad. In *eForth and Zen*, I didn't use real assembly code in 8086eForth, but used Bill Muench's original Forth code, which was more concise than the assembly code. This time I will use real MSP430G2 assembly source code of 430eForth v4.3, in this book.

The eForth commands were reduced from 223 to 182. From the remaining commands, headers of commands not used in programming were also removed, so that only 125 commands are visible to you. I think this is the minimal set of Forth commands you must learn, if you wanted to do serious, substantial programming. The headers of the invisible commands were only commented out, so that if you like, you can restore all the headers of all commands. You have to be careful with the link fields. I linked the dictionary manually, because I always had trouble with macros in various brands of macro assemblers which didn't do macros correctly as advised.

I was bit in love with the MSP430G2 and tried to optimize as many compound commands to become the tightest primitive commands. For example, all the binary ALU commands were reduced to two machine instructions:

```
PLUS:      add      @stack+,tos
$NEXT
```

MSP430G2553 is a nice little Forth Virtual Machine. MSP430G2 LaunchPad is a nice little computer you can do interesting applications in Forth. 430eForth v4.3 is my best efforts in giving you a lead to master the 2553 chip, leaving the smallest footprints in the flash memory and in your brain.

430eForth-IDE is the best companion of 430eForth v4.3. It replaces the very complicated conventional IDE tool chains like TI's Code Composer Studio and others. It integrates a terminal emulator, a flash downloader, a text editor, a file downloader, and many tutorial lessons, in a very small package. It is an excellent platform for young students to learn the Forth language. However, it is not a toy system. It is also useful for experience firmware engineers to write substantial applications, limited only by the 16 KB of flash memory in MSP430G2553 chip. I am probing the limits what this $4.30 LaunchPad can reach. I am coding my understanding of this chip and the Forth language into this kit, to enable you to reach the same level of understanding, and perhaps, enlightenment.

This is Zen, to understand a microcontroller with the least amount of money, time, hardware, software, and neurons.

Chapter 2. 430eForth-IDE on LaunchPad

As you might have noticed, in this book, the main text is in Times New Roman type. Computer input and output text is in Courier New type. Books and references are Italic. Forth commands and assembly instructions are also in Courier New type, when they are embedded in main text.

2.1 430eForth-IDE

When I first ported eForth to MSP430G2553 on the LaunchPad Kit, I had to have the following tools:

- A MSP430G2 LaunchPad Kit with an USB cable connecting to PC.
- A Windows PC to load Code Composer from TI Corp
- A terminal emulator on PC to communicate with LaunchPad

Code Composer Studio contains an MSP430 assembler, C and C++ compilers, an editor to enter source code, and an on-line debugger to debug your program. The editor was nice, and it displays words in color according to syntax. The assembler was claimed to be a macro assembler, but it didn't do string arguments correctly, and it didn't support assembly variables.

There are worse assemblers than this one, but I managed to get it to produce the code I wanted. The debugger downloads assembled object code to MSP430G2553 through the USB cable. It does single stepping nicely, but the break points never broke. It was disappointing, but I learnt to synthesize my own break points. Eventually I could flush out all the bugs and got many versions of 430eForth to work.

Once I got a working version of 430eForth, I only needed CCS to download the object file to MSP430G2553. After that, all programming and debugging operations are done through the terminal emulator on PC.

On the PC, I used to have HyperTerminal to communicate with target microcontrollers. HyperTerminal was bundled with Windows prior to Windows 7. Starting at Windows 7, Microsoft stopped bundling it with Windows. However, you can still download HyperTerminal executable file from MSDN website. There are other terminal emulators like RealTerm which can be downloaded from SourceForge
(http://realterm.sourceforge.net/).

CCS is a huge beast. Its footprint on my PC is 1.2GB. Nowadays, GB is cheap, but for the functionality I am using, it is too big. I have better use of my disk. It is also very complicated, and I spent lots of time trying to figure out how to get it to produce listing files, hex files and object code I wanted. However, once it started to produce a correct object file, every misdeed was forgiven. And then, I wondered, did I really need such a huge system just to download 4KB of object code to LaunchPad?

Now, all you need is 430eForth-IDE to experiment 430eForth, and develop substantial application. LaunchPad and 430eForth-IDE. Can it be any simpler?

430eForth-IDE was a gift from Dirk Bruehl with www.4E4th.org. It replaces the very complicated CCS IDE and an extra terminal emulator. It can flash (download) 430eForth object code directly to the flash memory in LaunchPad, and communicates with 430eForth through its terminal emulator. It has a nice text editor to write Forth source code into text files, and it can download text files to compile applications on the LaunchPad. In a very small package, it provides all the services I need for firmware engineering. The complete IDE with 430eForth object file can be downloaded for free at:

http://www.somersetweb.com/430eForth/430eForth-IDE.zip

and

http://wiki.forth-ev.de/doku.php/en:projects:430eforth:start

This is Zen of LaunchPad. The smallest, the simplest, easiest, and the most pleasant firmware engineering system, free to all.

The object code file 430eForth.a43, which is in Intel Hex Format, can be flashed to LaunchPad whenever you are in trouble. It also has the LaunchPad USB driver in case the USB connection between LaunchPad and PC is broken for whatever reason. It also has many sample Forth source code files and lessons you can try and learn from.

In this chapter, I will show you how to get 430eForth-IDE to work. In Chapter 3, I will show you how to assemble 430eForth.asm, using CCS IDE tools. In Chapter 4, I will explain 430eForth.asm in its glorious details. My goal is to pass on to you the understanding and the enjoyments I had in LaunchPad. Hopefully, you will get enlightened and see the Zen of it.

2.2 LaunchPad Adjustments

Starting with Rev1.5, TI's LaunchPad has jumpers to switch RXD and TXD pins between Software USART and Hardware USART. The TXD and RXD jumpers on J3 on the LaunchPad board are in software USART position when delivered by TI. 430eForth uses the hardware USART, so position of the TXD and RXD jumpers on J3 must be switched to horizontal positions as shown on the right hand side in the following picture. In case you are still using 430eForth with an older LaunchPad version 1.4, remove the TXD and RXD jumpers and re-connect the TXD and RXD pins crosswise, as shown on the left hand side in the following picture:

Dirk prepared a nice 12 step program to bring up 4E4th on a LaunchPad. It applies equally well for you to bring up 430eForth. You have to first install 430eForth-IDE on your PC, with Windows XP or Windows 7, and you need of course a LaunchPad with a MSP430G2553 chip.

1 Start Windows PC and 430eForth-IDE for Windows.

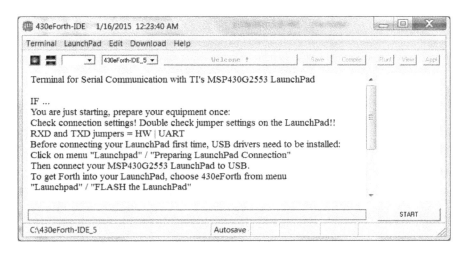

2 Unpack MSP430-LaunchPad: cut foil,

take out circuit board and take out USB-Cable
hidden under cardboard cover.

1   Check HW | UART position of RX/TX-Jumper, turn by 90° if necessary.

2   Connect USB-Cable out of MSP430-LaunchPad box to the MSP430-LaunchPad.

3   Connect USB-Cable to PC - green Power-LED lights, red and green LEDs blink.

4   MSP430 Application UART Hardware Wizard appears on screen. If not already
    set, click on
    Install Software automatically.
    Click on button Next - it will need some time till the software is found.

5   A message will come up telling the MSP430 Application UART has not passed
    Windows Logo testing to verify its compatibility with Windows. Click on button
    Continue Anyway.
    Installation will need some seconds.
    Click on button Finish.

6   Some messages are coming, telling that hardware
    is ready for use. Proceed with 430eForth–IDE.

7   Click on 430eForth–IDE Menu

LaunchPad>Preparing LaunchPad Connection.

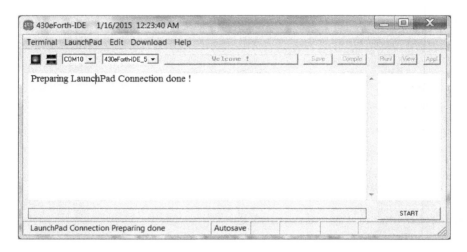

8   Click on 430eForth–IDE Menu
    LaunchPad>FLASH
    the LaunchPad> 430eForth.a43

9   Popup warning message
    All your Forth Words will be lost.
    Proceed with FLASHING the 430eForth?
    Click on button Yes.

10 Flashing needs several seconds, when ready, message
    Flashing 430eForth done
    –checking connections now
    shows up. If everything is okay, the message:
    430eForthFLASH connections checked !
    Click 'Start' button to connect to target !
    shows up. Now 430eForth is installed on the LaunchPad!

The red and the green LED are lit as long as the LaunchPad

is connected to the PC and no program switched them off.

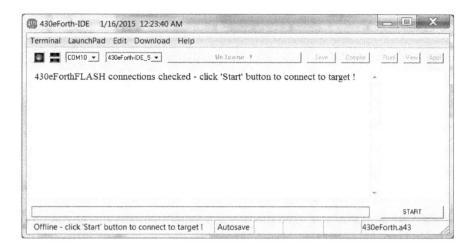

2.3 Trying 430eForth on LaunchPad

Bring up 430eForth-IDE on your PC. Connect your LaunchPad Kit board to a USB port on your PC. Flash or download its 430eForth.a43 file to LaunchPad Kit. Click the START button on lower right of the IDE screen. Reset LaunchPad and you get the sign-on message:

430eForth v4.3

After bringing up 430eForth, press <enter> key on the keyboard several times, and each time you will get a new line with an ok message. Now, with Caps Lock set on the keyboard, type:

WORDS <enter>

and you will see a list of eForth commands on the terminal:

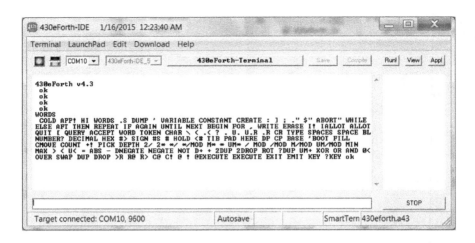

Every line of commands you typed in must be terminated by the <enter> key. I will not remind you this <enter> key again. The <enter> key causes 430eForth to interpret the line you just typed in. Before you press the <enter> key, you can back up the cursor and erase characters you typed, from right to left, and edit the text before pressing <enter>.

IDE breaks up a word at the right margin of the terminal. You will have to read across lines to see whole words. There are 125 Forth commands visible in 430eForth v4.3. These eForth commands are documented in the Appendix for your reference.

These are commands you can type and get the LaunchPad to do interesting things. Learn these commands and you will be the master over LaunchPad. These commands define the simplest version of Forth language, as implemented in 430eForth v.4.3.

What Forth Does for You But Nobody Else Can?

What can Forth do over C language and just about everything else?

One quick answer I can give you is to ask you typing in the following command:

```
HEX
0 DUMP
```

and you will see the following display in the terminal:

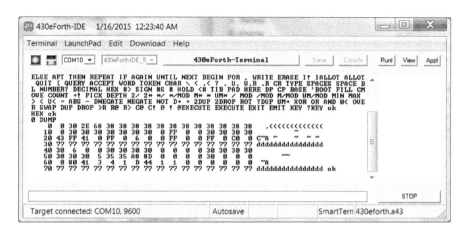

Lots of 7 characters. Not very interesting, erh? But, in this display, you see the RAM memory of MSP430G2 from location 0 to location $7F. If you had read the *MSP430x2xx Family User's Guide* carefully, you would know that the first 512 bytes in the memory space contain all the I/O registers. Many of these registers are not implemented as physical devices, and they show up containing $77. Actual I/O registers show their actual contents.

You can examine the contents of every I/O register any time. You cannot do it in C, unless you write a memory dump program. And then, it cannot do anything else.

You can dump other memory areas in MSP430G2553. RAM from 0 to $3FF, flash memory from $C000-$FFFF, and Information flash memory from $1000-$10FF. If you care about the Bootstrap Loader (BSL), it is from $C00 to $FFF. Don't ask me what or how BSL does things, but it is there for you to see. Try to DUMP other areas of memory. Get yourself familiar with its memory map. See if you can recognize information stored in different memory locations. Now is a good time to read Section 1.4 on Address Space in *MSP430x2xx Family User's Guide*.

You can read I/O registers and memory with DUMP command. Even better, you can change the contents of the I/O registers and RAM memory! You can crash the LaunchPad, I mean logically not physically, if you advertently change some of the critical I/O registers. However, there is no better way to understand the I/O devices in MSP430G2 than to read the I/O registers and the bits in these registers, and to change these bits while observing the signals coming out of the corresponding I/O pins. If you crashed LauchPad, just reach out and press the reset button, and eForth will appear again.

Once you understand the control, status, and data registers in an I/O device, you can write a short Forth command to exercise this device the way you eventually will use it. This command to test the device will grow to be a part of your application.

In the following sections, I will show you how to change some of the I/O registers directly to operate several I/O devices. You need that thick *MSP430x2xx Family User's Guide* opened on your desktop, and read the register definitions to follow the discussions. I will show you some I/O registers, and bits in these registers I use.

It is difficult at first to read register addresses and contents in hex, or hexadecimal, but I hope you will get used to them. The hallmark of a firmware engineer is that he reads hex numbers. It will be very rewarding when you can relate the hex digits with binary bits, and to have these bits actually do work and produce results you can observe visually.

Another important reminder. 430eForth is case sensitive and all its native commands are in upper cases. You better press the Caps Lock key now on your keyboard to make sure you are typing upper case characters. If you try to mix in any lower case characters, 430eForth will echo the incorrect name with a "?" error message in the place of the ok message. However, when you define your new commands, you can mix different case characters, but you have to be consistent with yourself.

The best way to wade through this thick *MSP430x2xx Family User's Guide* is to test the devices interactively with 430eForth.

OK. Here are the 430eForth game rules:

- **Commands and numbers must be separated by one or more spaces.**
- **A line of commands must be terminated by <enter>.**
- **Always type HEX at least once to enable hexadecimal numbers.**
- **Always type upper case characters. Use Caps Lock.**
- **Always open** *MSP430x2xx Family User's Guide* **on your desktop.**
- **\ starts a comment to end-of-line. Ignore it and following text.**
- **Parentheses (<text>) enclose a comment. Ignore them.**

Are you ready?

The Almighty C! Command

C! (spelled see-store") is the most powerful command in eForth for LaunchPad. It takes two parameters: a byte data followed by an address into which the data is stored. We will use this command alone in the first two experiments. It directly manipulates the GPIO registers in MSP430G2553 chip to drive output pins in the P1 port. Note that data and addresses of registers are all in hexadecimal. In eForth, a hexadecimal number generally has a $ prefix. However, after executing HEX command, all numbers are assumed to be hexadecimal, and you do not have to prefix them with the $ character.

Turn LEDs On and Off

The first device I will discuss is the GPIO port P1, because it drives the two LED's on LaunchPad, and also monitors the switch S1. Before you do the experiments, read about the control registers for P1 port. All 8 I/O pins of P1 ports are brought to the J1 and J2 sockets. The red LED is connected to P1.0 pin, the green LED to P1.6 pin, and S1 switch to P1.3 pin. P1 is a general purpose I/O device. We will be interested in only these 3 registers:

Address	Register	Name	Function
$20	P1IN	Input register	Status of input pins
$21	P1OUT	Output register	Output data
$22	P1DIR	Direction register	1: output; 0: input

Setting a bit in P1DIR register makes the corresponding pin an output pin. You do not have to change this register, because it was initialized properly on boot up. Then, writing this bit in P1OUT register sends it to its output pin. It is very easy to turn the LED's connected to P1.0 and P1.6 on and off by the following commands:

```
HEX
1    21   C!      \ Turn on red LED
40   21   C!      \ Turn on green LED
41   21   C!      \ Turn on both LEDs
0    21   C!      \ Turn off both LEDs
```

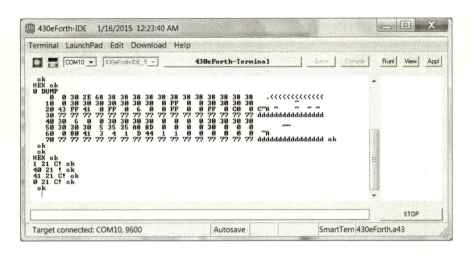

Type 'o DUMP' commands and you can see the current state of these registers as you turn the LEDs on and off. Note that memory location $20 also reflects the state of P1.0 and P1.6 as they are set or reset in location $21.

As you can see, memory location $22 is already set to $41. P1.0 and P1.6 were set to be output pins when 430eForth boots up.

Blink the LEDs

Now, we can write a small program to blink these LED's. Here is the program in eForth:

```
HEX
: ON   41 21 C! ;
: OFF  0 21 C! ;
: SEC   400 FOR 400 FOR NEXT NEXT ;
: BLINK  BEGIN ON SEC OFF SEC AGAIN ;
BLINK
```

As it is the first program you do in Forth, type these commands carefully. All Forth commands are separated by one or more spaces. Do not concatenate commands like BASIC programmers do. If two commands are not separated by a space, Forth would consider it single commands and gives you an error message with the offending command and a "?" mark. Don't worry. Just start over again until you get them right. The primary syntax rule in Forth is: Commands must be separated by spaces.

In the last section, we did type 41 21 C! to turn on the LEDs. Give these commands a name ON. We also did 0 21 C! to turn off the LEDs. Give these commands another name OFF. Now we have two new commands with names we all understand.

$400 is 1K in decimal. SEC does 1M cycles of empty loops, which take about 1 second. Execute BLINK will cause the LEDs to blink forever.

BLINK is the first program every LaunchPad user runs, in any programming language. It gives you a warm and fuzzy feeling that you are making LaunchPad do something significant. However, the above BLINK program is the silliest program a Forth programmer would ever write. It is an infinite loop you cannot get out, unless you push the reset button or pull the USB plug off. LaunchPad is not made to run BLINK. It is much more powerful and much smarter than just turning two stupid LEDs on and off.

OK. Select LaunchPad>FLASH LaunchPad and start over.

A thoughtful Forth programmer would write this program instead:

```
HEX
: SEC   400 FOR 400 FOR NEXT NEXT ;
: ON   41 21 C! ;
: OFF  0 21 C! ;
: BLINK  BEGIN ON SEC OFF SEC ?KEY UNTIL DROP ;
BLINK
```

BLINK again blinks the LED forever as the earlier one. But, when you are tired of looking at these blinking LEDs, you can stop them by pressing any key on the keyboard. You can exit the loop by pressing any key. This is what the commands ?KEY UNTIL are for. They are the back door for you to escape the loop. Now, you regain control. You can type in other commands to the 430eForth system, and do other useful things.

These commands are collected in BLINK.4th file. If you have trouble typing them correctly, download it and try BLINK. However, I do insist that you learn to type these lines correctly. You will not be admitted to my firmware engineering class if you can't do it. That's not a tall order. If you haven't learnt typing in school, this is a good time to learn it and to be good at it. I don't mind if you type with one finger. LaunchPad doesn't know the difference.

In FIG community, we had an old saying: "If you can blink a LED, you can do anything." Now you've done BLINK. You can do anything.

Read S1 Switch

If a bit in P1DIR is cleared to 0, the corresponding pin becomes an input pin. P1.3 is such an input pin. On LaunchPad, this pin is pulled to Vcc by an external resister, and it is also connected to a push-button switch S1 with its other terminal grounded. If the switch is open, you will read a high on the input pin, because of the pull-up resister. If the switch is closed, you will read a low on the input pin. Read P1IN register with the C@ (spelled see-fetch) command:

```
20  C@  .   \ read P1IN and show its contents
20  C@  .   \ repeat with S1 on and off
```

C@ is the opposite command of C!. It takes an address as parameter, reads one byte from this memory location, and returns its value on the parameter stack. The command . (spelled dot) displays this value on the terminal.

Pins P1.4, P1.5 and P1.7 are all initialized as input pins, although without pull-up resistors. You can use them as either input or output pins. Leave P1.1 and P1.2 alone. They are used by the USART com port.

GPIO port P2 has pins P2.0-P2.6 also brought to J1 and J2 sockets. You can use them as inputs or as outputs as you wish. Its control registers are:

Address	Register	Name	Function
$28	P2IN	Input register	Status of input pins
$29	P2OUT	Output register	Output data
$2A	P2DIR	Direction register	1: output; 0: input

GPIO ports P1 and P2 are much more complicated than what I showed above. I gave you the minimal amount of information, just to get you familiar with the commands C! and C@.

These are powerful commands which allow you to use LaunchPad to do many interesting experiments.

Tone Generator

MSP430 has two very powerful, and hence complicated, timer/counters. TIMER0_A3 and TIMER1_A3. They can be used as timers, counters, pulse width modulators, and square wave generators. Both timers have 16 bit counter registers, and many control registers to specify their exact operations. Here I will show you how to use Timer1 to generator audio tones. It is so simple. It will make you to want to throw that big, thick user's manual at whoever taught you firmware engineering.

MSP430G2553 chip has many I/O devices and not enough pins. So, each I/O pin in P1 and P2 ports is multiplexed to support several different devices. Each port has two selection registers to define the exact functions of its 8 I/O pins:

Address	Register	Name
$26	P1SEL	P1 select register
$41	P1SEL2	P1 select 2 register
$2E	P2SEL	P2 select register
$42	P2SEL2	P2 select 2 register

How each I/O pin is selected for specific functions is hidden in an obscure *Data Sheet on MSP430G2x53/2x13 (Slas735f)*, pages 42–57. I stepped on it like a blind cat catching a dead mouse. After that, the document *MSP430x2xx Family User's Guide* appears to make sense.
It's telling the truth. Nothing but truth. If you know truth, then everything in it is crystal clear.

OK. I want to use one timer to produce one square wave, on one output pin, to drive one small 8 Ohm speaker. There are many choices. I picked Timer1 and use its TA1.0 output. Among the many choices of output pins, I picked P2.0, mainly because it does not affect pins already used in P1 port. To map TA1.0 output to pin P2.0, here are the commands:

```
HEX
1   2A   C!   ( select P2.0 as output pin )
1   2E   C!   ( select TA1.0 output to P2.0)
```

Now, I want to use Timer1 to send a continuous square wave to P2.0 pin to produce an audio tone. Connect one terminal of an 8 Ohm speaker to P2.0 on LaunchPad, and ground the other terminal, as shown in the following picture:

All the control registers in Timer1 are 16 bit registers. I have to use the ! (spelled store) command. ! is the big brother of the Almighty C!. It stores a 16 bit value into a memory or register location. Timer1 has registers in the locations from $180 to $196. To produce a simple square wave, I only use the following three registers:

Address	Register	Name	Function
$180	TA1CTL	TA1 control register	Select clock and timing mode
$182	TA1CCTL0	TA1 capture/ compare control 0 register	Select output mode
$192	TA1CCR0	TA1 capture/compare 0 register	Max counts to be compared

The bits in control registers TA1CTL and TA1CCTL0 are complicated, and you have to read the *User's Guide* to understand them. To run Counter0 in Timer1, TA1.0, as a free running counter, we select the toggling output mode in TA1CCTL0. Set the maximum counts to $1000 in TA1CCR0. Then start the counter using the SMCLK clock and up-count mode in TA1CTL register. Here are the commands:

```
80      182   !    ( Select toggling output mode )
1000    192   !    ( Set max count to 4096 )
210     180   !    \ Start counting up,
                   \ generate tone)
0       180   !    ( Stop counting)
```

Things just can't be any simpler. Right?

$1000 is 4K in decimal. With SMCLK running at 8 MHz, the tone generated is about 2 KHz. Change this value in TA1CCR0, and you can change the tone frequency at will.

There are two counter/timers, Timer0_A3 and Timer1_A3 in MSP430g2553. Each counter/timer has three compare/capture units, which can produce 3 different outputs, in continuous square waves, or PWM waves and others. The possibility is enormous. I can only lead you to the water. You have to do the drinking yourself.

The square waves are boring, like the blinking LEDs. Once you turn on the tone generator, it becomes irritating very quickly. Here I have a more interesting demo, a Morse Code Beacon. It requires some programming, though. It is in a file MorseCode.4th, originally written by Michael Kalus. But, I am getting ahead of myself. If you know how to download a Forth file in 430eForth-IDE, go ahead and try it. You just have to learn how to turn the tone generator on and off at the right time, and Morse code will beacon out automatically.

Two timers can produce two accurate square waves. That's a two voice electronic organ. I am sure, I can get two more voices with the rest of the 4 capture/compare units, and play Bach's 4 part organ music, although it is not a trivial exercise. An exercise left to the students.

You can use the commands:

```
180  DUMP
```

to see all the registers in Timer1, and many others. However, DUMP does not show the 16-bit registers properly, as it uses C@ to read memory in bytes. For some unknown reasons, MSP430G2 does not show 16-bit word values properly if you try to read bytes from it. I did try to dump 16-bit words, but then the byte registers do not show their values correctly. So, 430eForth dumps in bytes. You have to be aware that 16-bit registers show wrong values. To read the contents of a 16-bit register, use the @ (spelled fetch) and . (spelled dot) commands, or the ? (spelled query) command.

AD Converter

Analog to Digital Converter (ADC) is just about the most interesting, and probably the most complicated device in a microcontroller. MSP430G2553 chip has 11 channels of ADC to read analog signals from internal and external sources, making it extremely useful for real applications looking at real analog signals. However, from a programmer's point of view, ADC in MSP430G2553 is not very complicated, and we only have to worry about the following 4 registers:

Address	Register	Name	Function
$4A	ADC10AE0	Input enable register 0	Enable A0 to A7 input channels
$1B0	ADC10CTL0	Control register 0	Select reference, sample-hold, enable, and start conversion bits
$1B2	ADC10CTL1	Control register 1	Select input channel and clock divider
$1B4	ADC10MEM	Conversion memory register	ADC conversion results

MSP430G2 has an internal temperature sensor, connected to Channel 10 of the ADC device. In addition, a high reference voltage RF+ is connected to Channel 9, and a low reference voltage RF- is connected to Channel 8. Channel 11 is connected to (Vcc-Vss)/2. These internal analog signals are interesting because they allow us to test the ADC, without external circuitry to provide analog test signals. The lower Channels 0-7 are multiplexed on pins P1.0 to P1.7, very useful in analog applications.

On LaunchPad, Pin P1.7 is not used to do anything special, and we can assign it to A7 analog channel to do an experiment. P1.7 is defaulted to an input pin, and it is OK to use it for A7, with the following channel assignment commands:

```
HEX
80   4A   C!
```

To read the internal temperature sensor, type the following commands:

```
1A30 .1B0 !      ( clear ENC in ADC10CTL0 to set up ADC )
A0E0  1B2 !      ( select temperature sensor, clock/8 )
1A33  1B0 !      ( start ADC, 64 clocks for sample/hold)
1B4   ?          ( read and display results)
```

The results displayed are about $128 on this LaunchPad. If you have a warm finger, press it on MSP430G2553 chip and do 1A33 1B0 ! 1B4 ? to see if you can get a different temperature reading.

Here are commands which reads Channel 9, the high reference voltage RF+:

```
1A30 .1B0  !      ( clear ENC in ADC10CTL0 to set up ADC )
90E0 1B2   !      ( select low reference voltage RF- )
1A33 1B0   !      ( start ADC, 64 clocks for sample/hold)
1B4  ?            ( read and display results)
```

I got $B3. To read Chanel 8, the low reference voltage RF-:

```
1A30 .1B0  !      ( clear ENC in ADC10CTL0 to set up ADC )
80E0 1B2   !      ( select high reference voltage RF+ )
1A33 1B0   !      ( start ADC, 64 clocks for sample/hold)
1B4  ?            ( read and display results)
```

I got $1A4. OK. These are internal analog signals you can read. To read an external signal A7, let us connect Vcc to pin P1.7, and type the following command:

```
1A30 .1B0 !       ( clear ENC in ADC10CTL0 to set up ADC )
70E0 1B2  !       ( select external analog input on P1.7 )
1A33 1B0  !       ( start ADC, 64 clocks for sample/hold)
1B4  ?            ( read and display results)
```

I got $3FF. Connect ground to P1.7, and do the same 1A33 1B0 ! 1B4 ? , I got 3. You have to use a potentiometer to vary the input voltage between ground and Vcc. But, I will let you do the experiment yourself.

You must be wondering what is the meaning of numbers I stored into registers $1B0 and $1B2. All these bits are carefully documented in *MSP430x2xx Family User's Guide (Slau144i)*, from page 567-572. Let me just highlight some of the bits I touched.

Bit 1 in ADC10CTL0 is the ENC bit. This bit must be cleared before we can write new values into ADC10CTL0 and ADC10CTL1. Bit 0 is ADC10SC, which starts ADC conversion. These two bits were cleared when I first write $1A30 to ADC10CTL0 to clear ENC bit. After clearing ENC, I can write a $A0E0 to ADC10CTL1. The hex digit $A selects Channel 10 to read, and the digit $E sets the clock divider to 8 to slow down ADC conversion.

ADC10 converter has its own internal clock running at about 5 MHz. It is too fast to do ADC conversion at 200 KHz. Divide this clock by 8 seems to work. You may speed up this clock if you have time constrain in your application.

I first write $1A30 to ADC10CTL0. The Bits 15-13 are all 0. They form the SREF field. A zero in SREF selects Vcc and GND as the limits of ADC conversions. The Bits 13-11 is called ADC10SHT field. Both bits are set to select 64 clocks for Sample and Hold Time for an ADC conversion. I choose the longest sample and hold time to make sure this thing works. You may try other values in your program.

Bit 9 (REFOUT) is set to turn on reference voltage output. Bit 5 (REFON) is set to turn on reference voltage. Bit 4 (ADC10ON) is set to turn on the ADC converter.

When ADC10CTL1 is setup correctly, writing a $1A33 to ADC10CTL0 configures the ADC, sets ENC bit to protect the control registers, and starts an ADC conversion. After that, I read the Conversion Memory Register at $1B4 to get the results of conversion. Kapish?

OK. Time to pause.

You may not fully agree with my Magic Number Approach, typing values and registers addresses in straight hexadecimal numbers. However, these numbers represent my understanding of the four I/O devices in MSP430, the GPIO ports P1 and P2, the counter/timer Timer1_A3, and the ADC converter ADC10. In these exercises, I hope that I have demonstrated that you can control these devices with only two Forth commands: the Almighty C! command and its big brother ! command.

This is Zen computing. You get your computer to work with the least amount of commands. Clearly, LaunchPad understands these numbers I typed in, and acts upon them correctly. I am trying to pass these understandings to you, and hope you will get enlightened by them.

A microcontroller is a computer surrounded by a bunch of I/O devices. Once you have a Forth embedded in the microcontroller, you can look around and find all the I/O devices and control them. You will be the controller of a microcontroller. An I/O device is a bunch of registers getting data in or out some I/O pins. Knowing what the bits in which registers are doing, you can be the master and the controller. The registers and the bits are overwhelming at first sight. But with Forth working inside the microcontroller, you can master them by bits and pieces. You do not have infinite time to learn all of them, but you always have time to know enough of them to do your applications, which are always finite and therefore doable in a finite time frame.

Forth allows you to reach the registers and the bits in them. Spend time meditating on them. A microcontroller understands only these bits and registers. After tinkling these bits in registers, you will learn how to make them to work as you wish. Then you make new commands operating on these bits and registers. Pick good names for these commands to convey your understanding, and you will develop a specialized language in the form of a growing set of commands. Eventually, you will reach a command, which is your application.

This is Forth. This is Zen. As it is applied to microcontrollers, it is firmware engineering.

2.4 Menu Options in 430eForth-IDE

Let us go back to 430eForth-IDE and show you all the functions built in this very powerful integrated development environment. It contains all the tools you will need to build and debug substantial applications. After you download the 430eForth-IDE.zip file, unzip it and double click the 430eForth-IDE.exe icon, you will see the following window opened on your desktop:

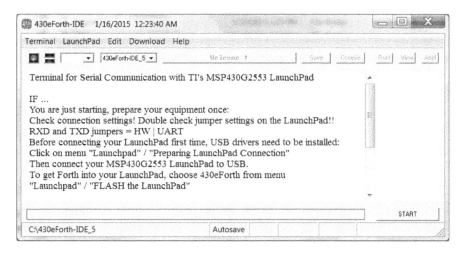

Follow the instructions in this window to install USB driver, and connect LaunchPad USB cable to your PC. If you do not have 430eForth v4.3 already installed in your LaunchPad, choose:
Launchpad>Flash the LaunchPad>430eForth.a43

The red LED  in the upper left corner shows that the 430eForth-IDE is in an Idle Mode not ready to communicate with the LaunchPad. To get connected with the target, click on the START button

START

in the lower right corner. The button changes to STOP and the IDE is in the Terminal Mode. The LEDs switch to green and you can start talking to LaunchPad.

An input panel at the bottom of the IDE screen allows you to type in Forth commands:

After you enter a character, it is echoed on the terminal panel in the middle. Typing a line of commands and pressing <enter> key on your keyboard send this line of text to LaunchPad for interpreting or compiling. The results of interpreting or compiling are shown in the terminal panel.

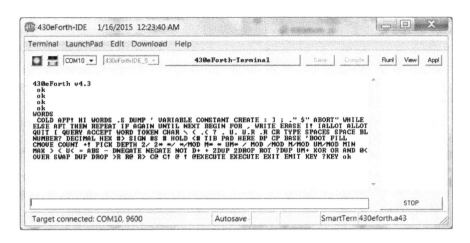

Now back to our description of the 430eForth-IDE menu options:

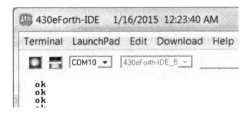

There are five different menus: Terminal, LaunchPad, Edit, Download, and Help.

Terminal Menu

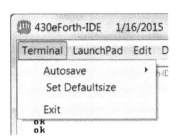

Terminal has three sub menus: Autosave, Set Defaultsize and Exit.

Terminal - Autosave

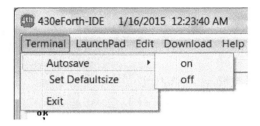

When a file download is done, all words are automatically saved, by executing a command sequence ' HI APP!. This is done to protect the commands just compiled into flash memory against an accidental reset, which clears the user variables but the new commands in the flash memory are not cleared. These commands left in flash memory will be overwritten in later compilations, and new commands will not be compiled correctly. If you executed these incorrectly compiled commands, anything could happen to the 2553 chip. To switch off this feature, click on Autosave off. This setting will be saved.

Terminal - Set Defaultsize

This option allows you to return to the default terminal size if you had adjusted it and wish to restore the default terminal.

Terminal - Exit

A click on Exit will end the 430eForth-IDE session. All entered data will be saved, starting 430eForth-IDE.exe anew will show the same data on terminal again after click on START. No data will be lost, but the Autosave, and terminal will be at default state again.

LaunchPad Menu

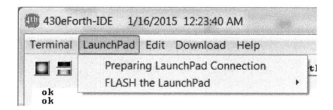

LaunchPad has two submenus: Preparing LaunchPad Connection, and FLASH the LaunchPad.

LaunchPad – Preparing LaunchPad Connection

Preparing LaunchPad Connection is needed when a LaunchPad is connected to a PC for the first time, see First Steps with 430eForth.

LaunchPad – FLASH the LaunchPad

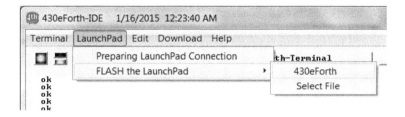

This menu FLASH the LaunchPad allows you to put 430eForth onto the LaunchPad, using one of these files which are residing in folder \Engine\Flasher. Flashing is done with a service program, and you will see a CMD window showing the flashing progress. Be patient, eventually, 430eForth will come back, checking the USB connection, and show you this screen:

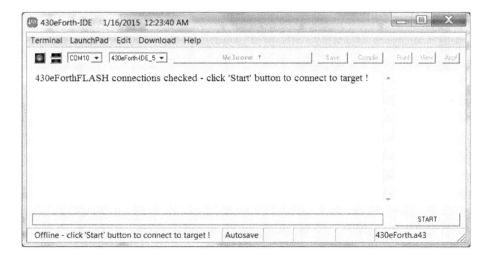

Flashing is successful, and you can press the START button to start using 430eForth-IDE. If flashing is not successful, check your hardware connections. Go back to Dirk Bruehl's 12 step start up process, as shown in Section 2.2.

Sometimes, closing 430eForth-IDE and restarting it helps.

Sometime, turning off PC and restarting it helps.

The worst case I encountered was that I had to replace the MSP430G2553 chip on LaunchPad, because somehow I managed to erase the protected Information Flash Memory Segment A, where TI stored the calibration constants for the Digitally Controller Oscillator (DCO). You don't have to be paranoid about them. But, if you do, record these constants from $10F8-$10FF, so that you can recover the chip if you accidentally erased them.

Edit Menu

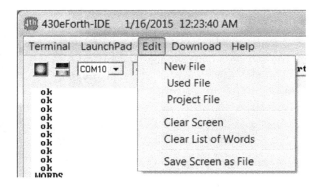

Edit menu has six submenus: New File, Used File, Project File, Clear Screen, Clear List of Words, and Save Screen as File.

Edit – New File

A click on Edit File opens a pop up window to allow editing the content of a selected 4th file on the 430eForth-IDE editing screen. IDE is changed to Edit Mode.

Edit – Used File

A click on Used File opens the most recently downloaded or edited file. IDE is changed to Edit Mode.

Edit – Project File

A click on Project File shows a list of all downloaded files, and a file can be selected for editing. IDE is changed to Edit Mode.

Edit – Clear Screen

A click on Clear Screen clears the terminal screen. When the screen buffer is full, IDE would seem to be unresponsive to terminal input. Clear Screen will get IDE to respond again.

Edit –Clear List of Words

A click on Clear List of Words clears the Word List Panel (right panel).

Edit –Save Screen as File

Save Screen as File opens a pop up window for you to save the current content of the 430eForth-IDE terminal screen. File extension will be attached automatically.

Download Menu

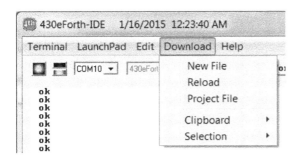

Download has five submenus: New File, Reload, Project File, Clipboard, and Selection.

Download - New File

A click on New File opens a pop up window to allow a file to be downloaded. Only 430eForth-Files and folders will be shown:

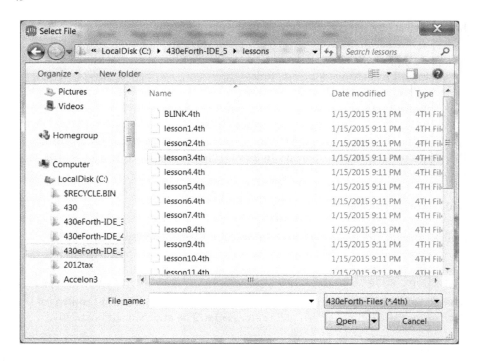

Download - Reload

A click on Reload opens and reload the most recently loaded or edited file.

Download - Project File

A click on Project File shows a list of all downloaded files, and a file can be selected for loading.

Download –Clipboard

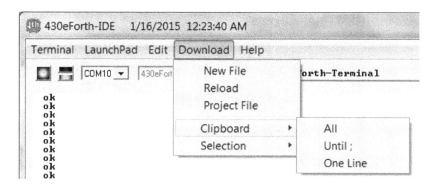

Download>Clipboard has three submenus: All, Until ; and One Line. They allow you to copy and paste words, programs, or part of a program. Simply copy the text you like to transfer to the target 430eForth, and click on Download>Clipboard>All in case you like to download the whole text at once.

There are two other options: A line by line download with a click on One Line or a download of a colon definition with a click on Until ;, repeating until all text is transferred. Click on button Next to proceed. A compile error will stop this download.

Download – Selection

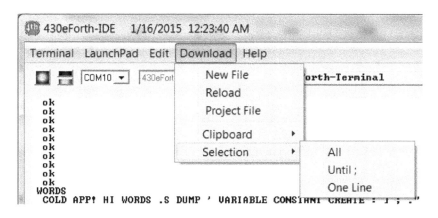

Download>Selection has three submenus: All, Until ; and One Line. They allow you to paste words, programs, or part of a program from the 430eForth-IDE screen. Simply mark these words on the 430eForth-IDE screen which you like to transfer to the target 430eForth, and click on Download>Selection>All in case you like to download the whole text at once.

There are two other options: A line by line download with a click on One Line or a download for one colon definition for each click on Until ;, until all text is transferred. Click on button Next to proceed. A compile error will stop this download.

Help-Menu

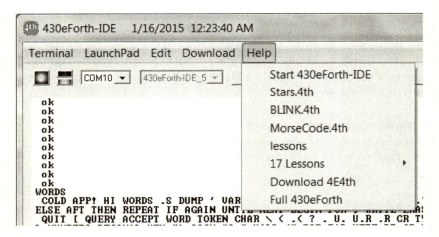

The Help menu has seven submenus: Start 430eForth-IDE, Stars.4th, BLINK.4th, MorseCode.4th, lessons, 17 Lessons, Download 4E4th, and Full 430eFirth.to help you with this 430-IDE and show you Forth programming examples.

Help – Start 430eForth-IDE

Clicking Start 430eForth-IDE opens a read-only window showing you the 12 steps to start 430eForth-IDE working, just in case you have trouble using this IDE.

Help – Stars.4th

Clicking Stars.4th opens a read-only window showing you the Stars.4th file. It is a simple Forth program you can type in or download it to compile.

Help – BLINK.4th

Clicking BLINK.4th opens a read-only window showing you the simple program to blink the red and green LEDs on LaunchPad.

Help – MorseCode.4th

Clicking MorseCode.4th opens a read-only window showing you a fairly long program to blink the red and green LED's and also beacon out Morse code from a small speaker.

Help – Lessons

The Help>lessons opens the lesson.4th file for you to practice editing and loading a large file with many errors to be corrected. If you were successful in getting this file to compile correctly, you would be on your way to be a successful Forth programmer. lesson.4th contains all 17 lessons included in 430eForth=IDE in a single file..

Help – 17 Lessons

The 17 Lessons were originally *The First Lessons* for FPC, and then ported to eForth. There are 17 lessons to show you how Forth programs are written, and the common style to compose Forth programs. These lessons are separated into 17 LessonXX.4th files so you can download and study them individually. Click on any of these files will open it in a separate read-only window. If you want to download them, click Download>Select File to select one of them. It you want to modify them, use the Edit menu.

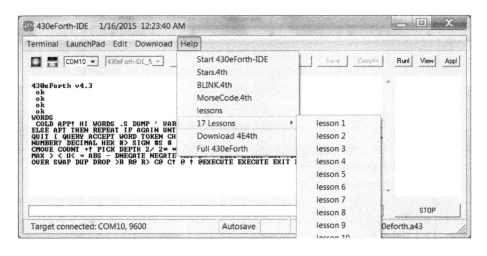

Help – Download 4E4th

Clicking Download 4E4th opens a read-only window showing you the website of www.4E4th.org, which distributes 4E4th, a Forth For Education system for students who are interesting in learning to use LaunchPad. 4E4th is derived from Brad Rodriguez's CamelForth, another implementation of Forth for LaunchPad.

Help – Full 430eForth

Clicking Full 430eForth opens a read-only window showing you the link to www.offete.com, from where you can buy a complete 430eForth system for $25. It includes assembly source and object files of 430eforth_9.asm, and a pdf file of this book.

eForth Lessons

If you are new to the Forth programming language or, has some prior knowledge on a different Forth system, you may want to look into a series of tutorials I prepared for this 430eForth systems. There are 17 lessons in that many text files. You are encouraged to take these lessons and type in the commands. You can also download these files in IDE, and then type in the final commands to test loaded commands. These lessonXX.4th files are included in the ..\430eForth-IDE\lessons folder.

A Stars.4th file will be used to demonstrate the integrated Editor and Compiler in Section 2.5. I added the BLINK.4th and MorseCode.4th as discussed in Section 2.2. A file lessons.4th contains all 17 lessons from an earlier eForth system. It has multiple line comments which cannot be compiled by 430eForth. It is used as an example to demonstrate the integrated Editor and Compiler in Section 2.5.

The contents of these lesson files are listed in the following table:

Lesson	Contents
1	Hello, World!
2.	Big characters
3.	Forth Interest Group
4.	Repeated patterns
5	The theory that Jack built
6	Help
7	Money exchange
8	Temperature conversion
9	Weather reporting
10	Multiplication table
11	Calendars
12	Sines and cosines
13	Square roots
14	Number conversion
15	ASCII character table
16	Random numbers
17	Guess a number
18	Stars.4th
19	BLINK.4th
20	MorseCode.4th
21	lessons.4th for editing exercises

2.5 Editing and Compiling in 430eForth-IDE

Originally, 4E4th-IDE - the Integrated Development Environment for MSP430 LaunchPad - , was packaged with 4E4th.a43 object file, which is a Forth system derived from Bradford J. Rodriguez' CamelForth for MSP430, and distributed by members of Forth Gesellschaft eV in Germany. The 4E4th-IDE is a Forth for Education (4E4th). It includes the 4E4th.a43 object file in Intel hex format, TI's LaunchPad_Driver.exe, MSP430Flasher.exe and TI's DLL's to boot 4E4th on the

MSP430 LaunchPad, and a terminal emulator to communicate with 4E4th via a virtual USB com port on PC.

4E4th, or MSP430 CamelForth is very similar to 430eForth. They are both minimalist Forth implementations, preserving the most essential commands to support an interpreter and a compiler. 4E4th claims to comply to ANSI Forth Standard. 430eForth deviates from the standard, in that it does not use the DO-LOOP structure, but uses the much simpler FOR-NEXT loop structure.

The reason? Chuck Moore once publicly apologized to the Forth community, that he misled us in adopting the DO-LOOP structure from FORTRAN. LOOP needs two parameters, an incrementing index and a limit, to decide whether to continue the loop or not. NEXT needs only one decrementing index, and can be implemented very conveniently in hardware.

Another difference between 4E4th and 430eForth is that 4E4th uses the Indirect Thread Model, while 430eForth uses a Direct Thread Model. The Direct Thread Model is simpler and faster.

Dirk Bruehl adapted 4E4th-IDE for my 430eForth system and called it 430eForth-IDE. It is a very nice companion of 430eForth v4.3, worthy of the name *Zen of LaunchPad*.

If you just start 430eForth-IDE, you generally get a terminal screen like the following:

In the 430eForth-IDE terminal window, there are three panels showing texts: The big panel in the middle and to the left is the Output Panel, showing text produced by LaunchPad. The narrow and long panel at the bottom is the Input Panel.

The Input Panel and Output panel are what we called a Terminal Emulator. They emulate an ADM3 Glass Terminal, or what we used to call a Dumb Terminal, which had a black & white CRT tube displaying 25 lines of 80 characters, and a keyboard, as shown below.

 If you are old enough, you might remember that in the 1970's, the Glass Terminals started to replace teletypes and big control consoles in the main frame computer control centers, and then spread out to laboratories and industries with minicomputers. When PC replaced minicomputers in the 1980's, they also replaced the Glass Terminals, which were relegated to computer museums and old programmer's memory.

The Glass Terminals had a USART (Universal Serial Asynchronous Receiver Transmitter) port to communicate with main frame and minicomputers. It needed only three wires for communication: a ground line, a transmit data TXD line and a receive data RXD line. It is the simplest communicating protocol among computers and other intelligent devices. Most microcontrollers retain one or more USART ports, but newer PC's opted for the USB ports. That's why we need a terminal emulator on PC to communicate with a microcontroller.

On the right side of the 430eForth-IDE terminal window is a Word List Panel. It displays the names of new Forth commands compiled into the 430eForth system. Commands selected from this panel are used by the three buttons just above the Word List Panel: Run!, View and APP!, which I will elaborate on later. These are very important services provided by 430eForth-IDE to help you test and debug new Forth commands as you write.

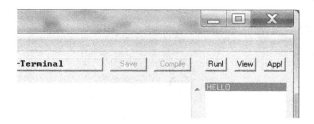

The START/STOP button in the lower right corner controls the working mode of the terminal window. When the button shows START, the terminal is in the Idle Mode. It encourages you to click it and enter into the Terminal Mode, to start talking to LaunchPad. Click START, and it changes to STOP, and the terminal is in the Terminal Mode, in which the terminal is communicating with LaunchPad. In the Idle Mode, the Input Panel is grayed out, and you cannot type into it.

In the Terminal Mode, the Input Panel is white, and it is ready to accept characters you type on your keyboard. The Input Panel accepts only one line of text at a time. Any character you type in the Input Panel is sent to LaunchPad, and LaunchPad echoes the character back, which is shown in the big Output Panel on the terminal.

In the Terminal Mode, you talk to LaunchPad directly. You type a line of commands and then press <enter> key to get LaunchPad to interpret the line you typed. The Input Panel allows you to edit this line of commands by Back Space or Delete key. Characters you typed will be faithfully echoed to the Output Panel. However, nothing is done until you press <enter> key.

Click STOP and the terminal changes to Idle Mode. STOP button changes to START. Now the Input Panel is grayed out and you cannot type in it. You can only scroll text up and down in the Output Panel. You can save all the text in a SaveFile.4th if you need the text for future use. You also have to be in the Idle Mode to flash a new object file to LaunchPad.

In either Idle or Terminal Mode, you can use menu EDIT>New File, Used File, or Project File to invoke 430eForth-IDE Editor to edit a file you select. The terminal changes to Edit Mode, showing the START button. When in Edit Mode, the long bar <430-eForth Terminal> changes to <Edit Selected File>. Now the file you selected appears in the main Output Panel, and you can edit its text just like in any other editor. Clicking the long <Edit Selected File> bar changes it back to <430-eForth Terminal> and vice versa.

I will come back to the Editor later. Right now, let us first explore the ways we write new Forth commands, get them compiled on LaunchPad, and debug them. 430eForth-IDE integrates all these services, so you can develop substantial programs without having to leave it and search for other tools. We will use this Stars.4th file to explore these different ways.

Let's first downloaded our Stars.4th file. Click Download>Select File, and select Stars.4th file from the pop-up selection window. The terminal screen looks like this:

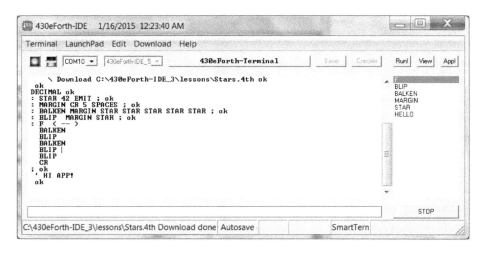

The second last line is ' HI APP! . These commands save all the current user variables to Flash Information Memory Segment D, so that all the new commands compiled from the file are available when LaunchPad is reset, or its power cycled. These Forth commands ' HI APP! are appended automatically each time after a file download is finished. It is important that you save the compiled commands before you turn off LaunchPad or push its reset button.

Otherwise, new commands will be compiled over the old commands left in the flash memory. You can crash the system if you try to execute the incorrectly compiled new commands. With ' HI APP! , you are protected from this mistake. However, this feature may be turned off by clicking Terminal>Autosave>Off. The status line at the bottom of the terminal shows Autosave, so this feature is active.

The last defined word was F, and this word is marked blue in the Word List Panel on the right side of the 430eForth-IDE.

There are three little buttons on top of the Word List Panel:

These buttons are used with the highlighted word in the Work List Panel. Let's first click on the first one, Run!. A click on Run! executes the command belonging to the marked word F, and shows the big letter "F" printed with * (stars):

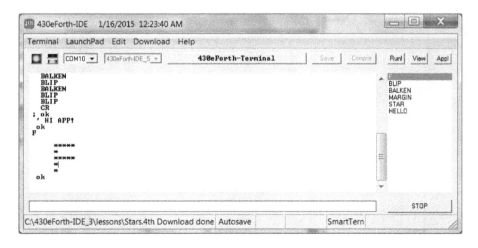

Click on the middle button View. The definition of F will be displayed on the

430eForth-IDE terminal Output Panel.

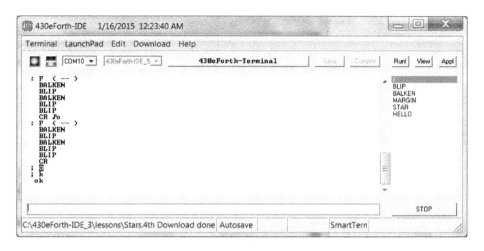

And last, but not least, click the third button, the most important one: App!

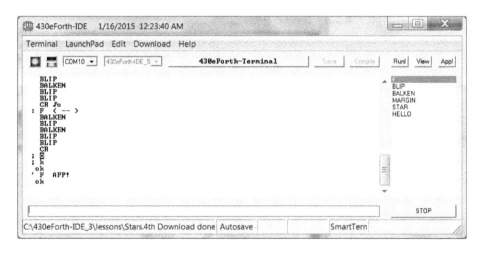

Normally you will use this button App! only when your program is finished, to save it and to tell the 430eForth-IDE that this marked command has to be executed with each reset or power on. To test this function, push the reset button on the LaunchPad, and here it is:

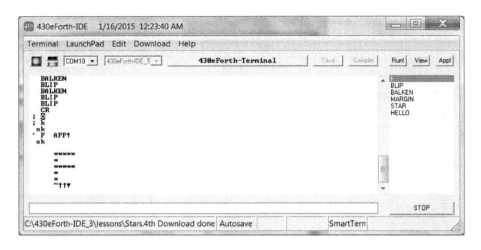

Look at the commands APP! button generated: ' F APP!. These commands are the TURNKEY service in firmware engineering terminology. It generates a microcontroller system which performs a function you specified on power up or reset. It is the final goal of firmware engineering, building a microcontroller system with a dedicated function.

Compiling with Copy/Paste

Open Stars.4th with our Editor by clinking Edit>New File, and select Stars.4th:

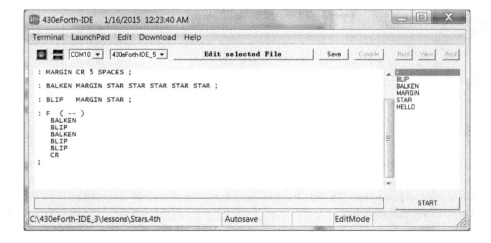

Select a portion of the text and copy it to the Windows clipboard with Ctrl-C:

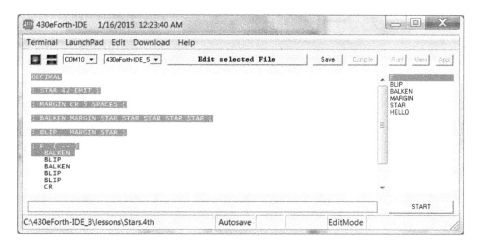

Click START button to turn the terminal to Terminal Mode. Then, click on Menu Download> Clipboard> Until ; . It sends all lines until the end of the first colon-definition to LaunchPad.

As you can see, button Run! is enabled, encouraging you to click it , and one other button Next is also enabled. A click on Run! starts the word STAR, which is marked in the Word List Panel, as usual:

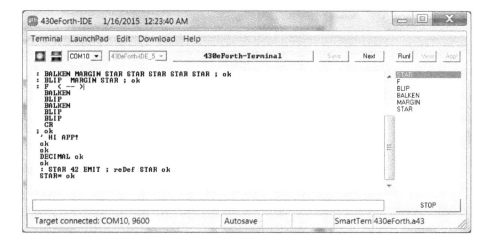

And several clicks on Next and Run! send the remaining copied text lines to LaunchPad:

As you can see, F is only partly defined, because you didn't copy the full file. I am sure you have been wondering why I asked you to do that. There was a reason for this. I like to show you another method to finish this definition.

It is really easy. Click on Run! again. And as a result, the word BLIP is added to F. Then mark or highlight the word BALKEN and click on Run! again. Highlight the word BLIP and click on Run! three more times. Here is what you see:

Typing the rest of the commands CR ; . Pressing <enter> key finally finishes the definition:

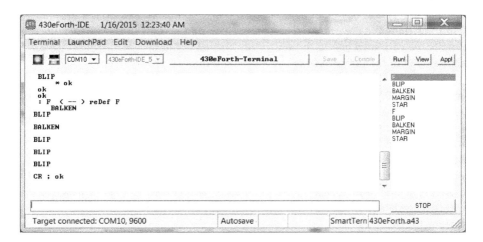

With another click on Run!, the newly defined command F is executed.

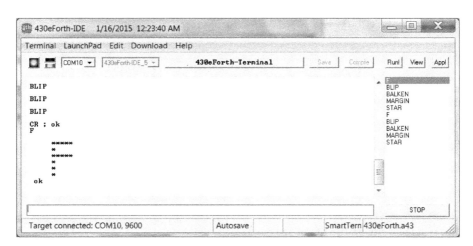

These examples show you that compiling with our 430eForth-IDE is much more convenient than by typing words on a standard terminal emulator.

2.6 Debugging in 430eForth-IDE

The Editor in 430eForth-IDE is no ordinary editor. It is intimately integrated with the compiler so that any error detected by the compiler is fed back to Editor. The Editor positions the file properly, so that you can fix the error immediately and compile the corrected text in the source file opened in Editor. Debugging is greatly facilitated with the integration of the Editor and the Compiler.

As an exercise for you to try, I have a lessons.4th file from an early eForth system. I combined all the lesson files together so that all the lessons could be loaded as a single file. I intended to demonstrate that a large application can be downloaded and compiled quickly. However, that early eForth system allowed comments within a pair of parentheses to be spread across many text lines. These comments will not compile correctly in 430eForth, which assumes that a comment stays in one line of text. It is a good debugging exercise to fix all these comments. If you succeeded in editing this file and compiling this file correctly, you would have mastered 430eForth-IDE.

OK. Download lessons.4th by clicking Download>Edit File, and select lessons.4th. LaunchPad compiles several lessons (examples) and encounters an error, showing the following error box:

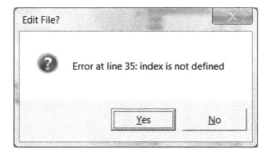

This error box sits on the top of the compiler screent:

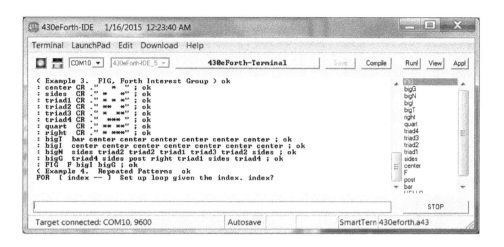

The last line of comments starts with:

```
FOR  [  index -- ]
```

FOR and [happen to be valid Forth commands and they pass the compiler, though not as I intended. However, index is not a valid command and generates the error.

Click Yes to dismiss this error box, and the terminal goes into Edit Mode and shows you the text where error occurred:

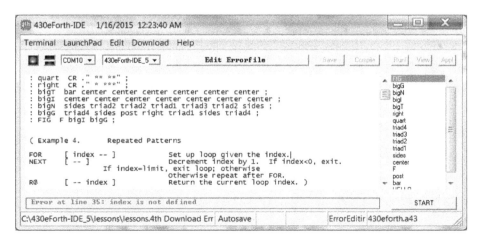

LaunchPad successfully compiled the first three lessons. Lesson4 (Example 4) started with a big comment that 430eForth cannot handle. The terminal is switched to Edit Mode and the text causing the error is shown in the middle of the screen. I will complete the first line of the comment with a closing parenthesis, and delete the rest of the comments, as follows:

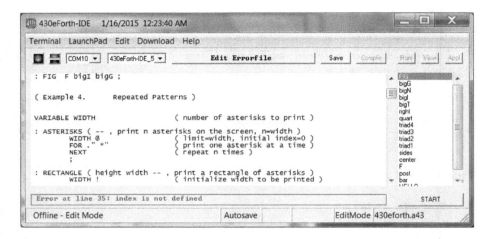

Click the now highlighted Save button, next to the long <Edit Error File> bar, and the edited file is saved to disk, and the Compile button next to it is highlighted. Click Compile button once to change Edit Mode to Terminal Mode:

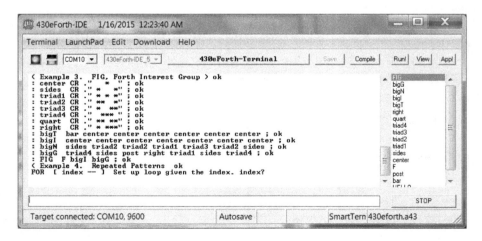

Click Compile button again to start compiling at the highlighted command FIG in the

Word List Panel. LaunchPad continues compiling until it encounters the next error, as shown here:

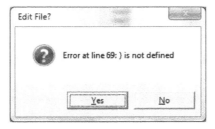

The terminal panel shows a triangle of stars:

Press Yes button on the error box, and the Edit panels shows where the error occurred. It is the last character in a 5-line comment:

(Try the following instructions

   3   10   **RECTANGLE**
   5   18   **PARALLELOGRAM**
  12   **TRIANGLE)**

The (command in the first line started a comment which was supposed to spread over 5 lines, but 430eForth only took in the first line as a comment, and tried to interpret or execute the next 4 lines as Forth commands. It interpreted the commands RECTANGLE, PARALLELOGRAM, and TRIANGLE correctly, and it encountered the character) , which is not a valid Forth command, but was placed there to terminate a comment.) was not a command, and it terminated the Forth interpreter with an error message)? , and 430eForth-IDE accordingly posted the error box.

Dismiss the error box, and the Edit panel shows this multiple line comment:

Delete this 5-line comment:

Press Save button to save the changes, and then press the Compile button to get back to the Terminal panel:

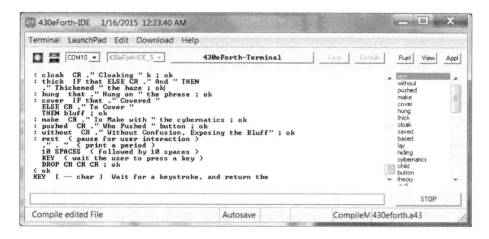

Press Compile button again to continue compiling. The next error box is as following:

In this multiple line comment, the first word is KEY, which is a valid Forth command. It is waiting for a key stroke from the keyboard. No key is pressed and the 430eForth-IDE receiver timed out and produced the ** Timeout COM ** error box. Dismiss this box and the Edit panel appears. Delete this multiple line comment:

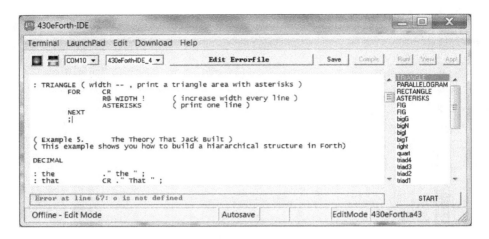

Continue this Edit-Save-Compile-Compile cycle until the entire file is edited and compiled correctly. All errors in the lessons.4th file are caused by multiple line comments, except that in Lesson13 (Example 13), the command CELLS was not defined in 430eForth and it causes an error. Changing CELLS to 2* does it. I only became completely comfortable with 430eForth-IDE after learnt this Edit-Save-Compile-Compile cycle. If you get through it, you will agree with me that 430eForth-IDE is the best Debugger/Editor/Compiler and firmware engineering tool for programming the LaunchPad Kit.

Now, let me summarize our discussions so far:

- LaunchPad gives you easy access to the MSP430G2553 chip.
- 430eForth v4.3 gives you a Forth language to program MSP430G25553.
- 430eForth-IDE gives you an integrated development environment to write, test, and debug applications.

Firmware engineering is now reduced to the bare minimum. This is what Zen masters struggled to achieve. The essence of things, and nothing else. Once you gain a complete understanding of this MSP430G2553 chip through 430eForth, it can be applied to all other microcontrollers. Enlightenment is here for you to grab.

Special acknowledgements to Dirk Bruehl who built this IDE long time ago for his Forth projects, and spent countless hours adapting it to 430eForth, accommodating many of my requests and wishes.

Chapter 3. Assembling 430eForth

3.1 Introduction

For a very long time, firmware engineering meant to program a UV Erasable PROM chip and to insert it on a board which contained a microprocessor, some RAM memory chips, and some I/O chips, and a socket for the UV EPROM. Then flash memory chips replace UV EPROM's. And then everything is integrated into a single microcontroller chip, and we now have ISP, In System Programming, which allows you to program the microcontroller in its own socket.

Nowadays, firmware engineering is synonymous to microcontroller programming. Since microcontrollers invaded every field of engineering and technology, and are embedded in every box in which electrons flow, firmware is everywhere. Firmware engineers never got the glory, but was the first people to be blamed if anything went wrong.

Hardware engineers built chips, assembled chips on boards, and assembled boards in boxes. Software engineers write software for main frame, minicomputers, and PC's, and the software runs in RAM memory. Firmware is software that cannot be changed easily. It is not as hard as hardware, and not as soft as software. So, firmware engineers are a different breed of engineers. They have to make sure that all hardware component work smoothly together, from the moment power is applied to the product, and the product work perfectly throughout its life cycle.

The goal of firmware engineering is to build perfect firmware. Failure is not an option. Where do you learn firmware engineering to build perfect firmware? I am not aware of any university offering firmware engineering degrees or courses. Yet, I saw this claim: "Firmware is the most expensive thing in the universe!" (*Augustine's Laws*, Norman Augustine, AIAA, 1997)

How can you write a perfect program? No, you can't. The industrial practice is to hire lots of testers to do lots of tests. You find bugs, and you fix the bugs. After you find enough bugs, you release the product and let the users test it. They will report bugs, and you fix them and make a new release. You can claim you have spent so many man–hours and fixed so many bugs, but you have no proof that your program is correct.

Forth is the only programming language in which you can prove the correctness of you program. You start from a microcontroller, and it is reasonable to assume that all the instructions in this microcontroller are correct. From this instruction set you can build a Forth Virtual Machine, with a limited set of commands which can be proven correct, by exhaustive testing. From this set of correct Forth commands, you build lists with finite members and finite pathways among them. These lists can be proven correct by exhaustive testing. These lists are made new commands, and are used to build lists at the next higher level. And so forth. Until you reach a final command as your application.

Forth allows you to build perfect programs. This is not fiction. All Forth programmers practice this methodology, and they had demonstrated time and again that they built large and reliable programs with less people working less time. Forth is the ideal language for microcontroller programming and firmware engineering. This is the message I like to pass on to you.

LaunchPad is the smallest and cheapest microcontroller kit that I have to teach Forth programming and firmware engineering. LaunchPad Kit integrates an MSP430G2553 microcontroller with all hardware components necessary to run Forth on a small printed circuit board, and it is good enough to train would-be firmware engineers and DIY hobbyists. After 20 years of implementing eForth on many different microcontrollers, I am certainly of the opinion that eForth is the Forth best suited for microcontrollers, and of course for LaunchPad.

The original eForth was implemented in Direct Thread Model by Bill Muench and myself. I took the original eforth86.asm file and modified it so it could be assembled by the MSP430 assembler in Code Composer Studio development system from TI. I call it 430eForth because it is configured specifically for MSP430G2553, used on LaunchPad Kit.

The most important features of 430eForth are the following:

- Direct Thread Model.
- Using byte addresses to access flash and RAM memory.
- All assembly source code is in a single 430eForth.asm file.
- New Forth commands are written directly to flash memory.
- No interrupts and no multitasking.
- Information flash memory Segment D is used to initialize use variables.
- Only 182 commands are retained.
- 125 commands have headers and can be used for programming.
- 83 commands are coded in assembly.
- Ease in building turnkey applications.

These features make 430eForth a very simple system, easy to use, easy to understand, and easy to modify. That's why this Forth is prefixed with an "e".

Things have changed since 1990, and things stay the same. Bill had the original eForth written in Forth. He helped me porting it to MSDOS on PC, using MASM from Microsoft. We didn't realize that MASM was the best macro assembler then and ever, and none of the later macro assemblers could match its macro capabilities. As I ported eForth to other microcontrollers, none of their macro assemblers handled string arguments to macros correctly, and very few had good assembly variables which could be changed as needed. Eventually, I hand coded the link fields and the name fields in all commands, so that the eForth implementation could be moved freely to any assembler with variable levels of macro capability.

TI released its Code Composer Suite (CCS), an integrated development environment, to support MSP430 LaunchPad, and other chips in the same family. The free version allows me to assemble code up to 16KB limit. It is fine for me, because most eForth needs only 6KB of code memory. For this 430eForth v4.3, I squeezed it down to about 4KB.

CCS is a huge suite, taking 1.2GB on my disk. It is also complicated, with lots of options to choose from. However, once you get used to it, and all its options, it works nicely.

3.2 Installing Tools

Here are the steps you can follow to get 430eForth assembled and running on LaunchPad.

Get an LaunchPad Kit board from DigiKey for $4.30. (Now about $10).

Download the Code Composer Studio from TI web site:
http://www.ti.com

Install Code Composer Studio. Do not connect the USB cable until the software installation is complete.

To check on these USB drivers, plug in the USB cable to PC from LaunchPad and go to

Start>Control Panel>System>Hardware>Device Manager>Ports (Com & LPT),

you will see MSP430 Application UART(COM X). Remember the COM port number X for use with a terminal emulator.

3.3 Assembling 430eForth

You have to be thoroughly familiar with Code Composer Studio in order to get it assembling 430eForth correctly and get it to work on LaunchPad. Follow the two CCS documents *Code Composer Studio v5.1 User's Guide for MSP430 (Slau157)* and *Code Composer Studio Development Tools v3.3 Getting Started Guide(Spru509)*. I will not repeat the steps that you must go through to get CCS up. I will only highlight the steps that are essential to get the 430eForth system assembled and running.

Code Composer Studio presents its window in Perspectives. A Perspective is a collection of panels showing relevant information about the project at certain stage of program development. The first perspective you use is the Edit Perspective, which contains a Project Navigation panel to the left, a text editing panel to the upper right, a Terminal panel at lower left, and a Problem panel at lower right. This is where you enter source code, edit your code, and assemble your code.

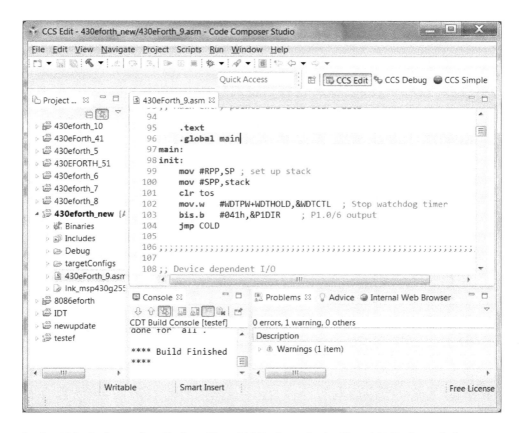

In the CCS window, select Project>New CCS Project. In the New CCS Project window, enter a project name, like 430eForth, in the Project Name box. A default path is shown in the Location panel. You can change this path by clicking the box to the right of Location panel, and then navigate to the folder you want.

Select MSP430G2553 as the Device.

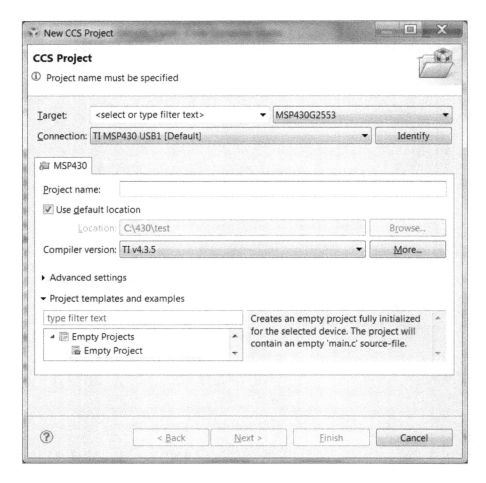

In the Advanced Setting Options, change Output Format from ELF to COEF. This is very important. If the assembler sends out an ELF file, the linker will not recognize it and produces a fatal error. No .out file will be produced and you will be stuck in a deep hole. At this point the New CCS Project window looks like the following:

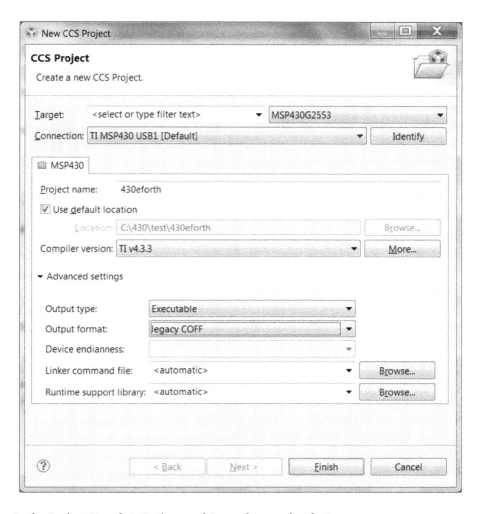

In the Project Template Options and Examples panel, select
Empty Projects>Empty Assembly-Only Project option and the
New CCS Project window looks like this:

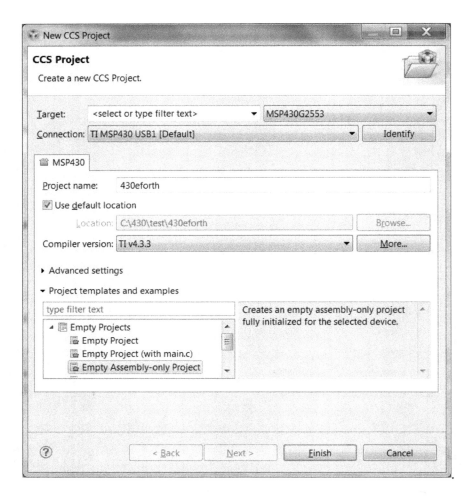

Click Finish button and the CCS Edit window shows you the new project. You are ready to go to work.

In the workspace folder CCS built for you, you will create a new project 430eForth in a new folder. Copy 430eForth_9.asm into this folder, and open this file in the Edit perspective. The CCS window appears like the following:

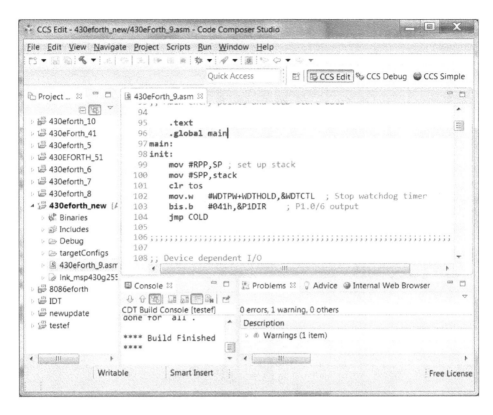

Pull down the Project menu and select the Build All option. CCS starts assembling 430eForth.asm, and displays lots of messages in the Terminal panel at the bottom of the Edit panel. Its final message is: Build Finished. Scroll up the Terminal panel, and you will see the most important message:
'Finished building target: 430eForth.out'

Assembling is successful. However, above it there is 1 warning. In the Problems panel to the right, it also shows the results: 0 error, 1 warnings, 0 others. The linker does not find the entry point and is not happy. Ignore the warning. If you are curious, you can Google the text warning# 10202–D, and find out its meaning. In fact, I don't know what it means, and I had not found the way to eliminate it. It doesn't seem to hurt. It there are error messages, you will have to correct the mistakes until the linker produces a .out file.

3.4 Other Project Properties Options

You got 430eForth to assemble correctly. It is a great step forward. However, there are many other options to select, and to set up the debugger so that you can download the object code to LaunchPad and get the 430eForth system up to talk to you.

Generating a Listing File

It is important to generate an assembly listing file so you can see how your assembly source is translated into machine instructions. When the assembler encounters an error, the error is usually reported in more details at the end of the listing file. Follow this links:

Build>MSP430 Compiler>Advanced Options>Assembler Options
Check Generate listing file:

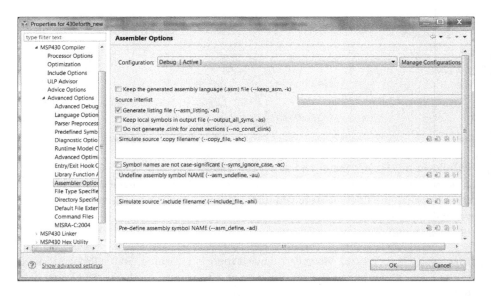

Enable MSP430 Hex Utility

CCS normally produces an object file .out for the debugger to flash into LaunchPad. However, many other tools like 430eForth–IDE needs object file in Intel Hex format. You have to ask CCS politely to give it to you in the right format.

MSP430 Hex Utilities>

Check Enable MSP430Hex Utility

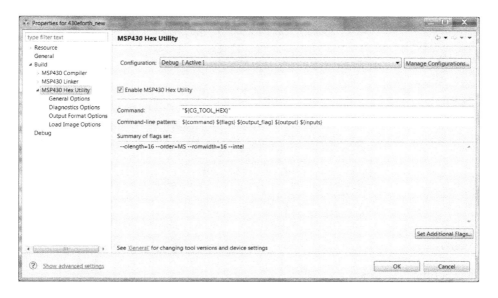

Select Intel Hex Format

MSP430 Hex Utilities>General Options

Select 16 data items per line of hex output

Specify MS data ordering

Specify 16 for ROM width

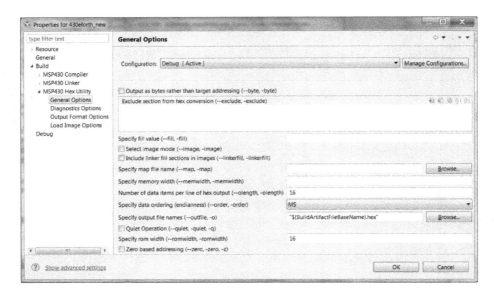

Select Intel Hex Output

MSP430 Hex Utilities>Output Format Options
Select Intel Hex format

CCS generate a .hex file if you select the Intel Hex Output. This file is identical to the .a43 file format required by 430eForth-IDE. Change its extension from .hex to .a43 and 430eForth-IDE will be pleased to accept it.

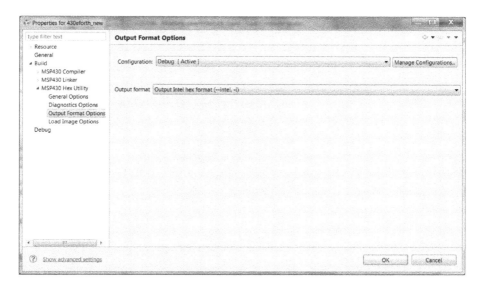

Erase Main and Information Memory

430eForth stores the initial values of its user variables in Information Flash Memory Segment D. You have to let the debugger to store these values in the otherwise protected Information Memory. Otherwise, Debug will complain and will not flash the memory, because it normally is not allowed to erase and write the Information Memory.

Debug>MSP430 Properties>Download Options>Erase Option
Check Erase main and information memory

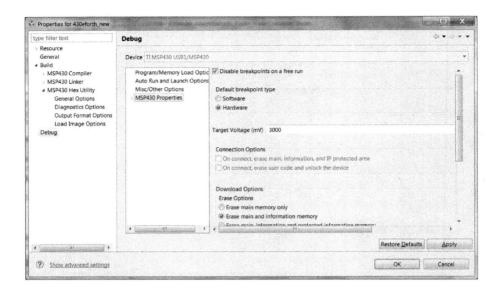

3.5 Download and Debug

Getting all the options selected correctly, then go back to the Edit Perspective.

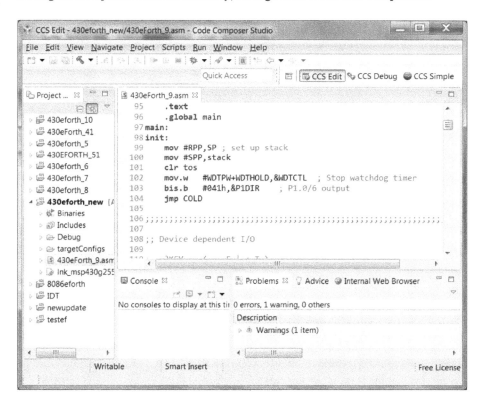

Click Run>Debug option. You are now presented with a Debug Perspective, where you can test, debug and run 430eForth. In the following figure I show you my favorite Debug Perspective panels.   The Debug panel is at upper left.   The Registers/Breakpoints panel is at upper right. The Edit panel is at lower left. The Memory/Disassembly is at lower right.

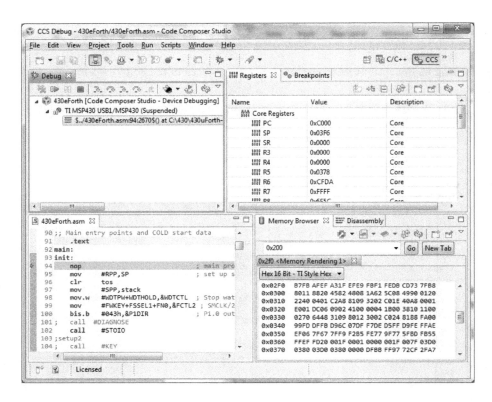

Click Debug>Run, and you are sent to the Debug Perspective, after CCS changes thing around and also download the object file to LaunchPad. It will take about 10 seconds. In one of the pop-up windows, it tells you how many bytes are in the object image. Finally, the Debug Perspective appears:

In the Debug panel, the tool bar contains 12 buttons, since I cannot draw these icons, I just list the buttons and show you what they do:

1. Remove all terminated launches
2. Resume
3. Suspend
4. Terminate
5. Step Into
6. Step Over
7. Assembly Step Into
8. Assembly Step Over
9. Step Return

10. Reset
11. Restart
12. Refresh

I mostly use Resume to start running, Suspend to stop running, and Terminate to stop debugging and return to the Edit Perspective.

When debugging, I use Assembly Step Into and Assembly Step Over. In the Registers panel, I always display registers R0 to R6, as R4 is tos (Top of parameter stack), R5 is the parameter stack pointer stack, and R6 is the interpret pointer ip. In the Memory panel, I generally display RAM memory from $360 to $3FF. The return stack is from $3F8 down, and the parameter stack is from $378 down. Watching the parameter stack generally allows me to find problems and ways to correct them.

OK. In the Edit panel, the line of code after main is highlighted, showing the first instruction about to be executed. You can click the Assembly Step Into buttons to step through the code. Do a few steps, and watch the changes in the registers as instructions are executed.

Since 430eForth v4.3 is fairly well debugged, you can click the Resume button to run it. If you have the 430eForth-IDE open, you will see the sign-on message on the terminal Output Panel:

Now you can go back to Chapter 2, and do all the exercises and learn all the lessons. Then, you will be on your own, perhaps start your own project.

Chapter 4. 430eForth Source Code

MSP430G2553 is a very interesting and capable microcontroller from TI Corp. It has a 16 bit CPU with 16 registers, 16 KB of flash memory, 512 bytes of RAM memory, 256 bytes of flash information memory, and a host of I/O devices. It is produced in a 20 pin DIP package, with 14 I/O pins. It is ideally suitable for many embedded applications. Being a 16-bit CPU, it is a very good host for a Virtual Forth Machine.

The original eForth Model Bill Muench and I developed in 1990 for 8086 and 8051 used the Direct Thread Model which was successfully ported to many different microcontrollers. The Direct Forth Model was used primary for portability, because the high level compound commands can be ported to other microcontroller without modification, as the token lists in them are simple lists of execution addresses. Most microcontroller assemblers could assemble the address lists identically. Only the low level primitive commands had to be re-coded for the particular microcontroller.

In spite of its many shortcomings, MSP430G2 is a good host for a Forth Virtual Machine. A very special feature in MSP430G2 makes it especially suitable for a Forth Virtual Machine, an indirect auto-increment memory read mode. It allows the $NEXT macro instruction to be reduced to a single machine instruction mov @ip+,pc, This single feature pushes the performance and the code density of direct thread model above both the indirect thread model and the subroutine thread model. Hence, in 430eForth v4.3, I adopt the Direct Threading Model.

In the direct thread model, a primitive command contains a sequence of machine instructions, terminated by a macro $NEXT, which is a machine instruction mov @ip+, pc. In a compound command, the token list is preceded by a macro $NEST, which is a call DOLST instruction. DOLST starts interpreting the following current token list. The last token in a token list must be $EXIT, which resumes the unfinished previous token list, from which the current list was called. $NEXT, $NEST, and $EXIT are the inner interpreters which process deeply nested token lists quickly and correctly, and they are expressed most efficiently in the direct thread model.

The CPU stack pointer register R1 (sp) is used as the return stack pointer in the Virtual Forth Machine for nesting and unnesting token lists. The register R5 is used as the parameter stack pointer stack. Both the return stack and the parameter stack are located in the high end of the RAM memory. The top element of the parameter stack is cached in register R4, called tos, and it significantly increases the speed in accessing the parameter stack. Register R6 is used as an interpret pointer ip, to scan token lists.

Besides the stacks, the RAM memory area also contains 12 user variables, a terminal input buffer, a word buffer to parse input strings, and a number buffer to build numeric strings for output.

In the original eForth Model, only 31 primitive commands were coded in machine instructions to enhance its portability to a wide range of microcontrollers. In the 430eForth v4.3, to make it run faster, 83 commands are re-written in MSP430 machine instructions.

In the following sections, I will present the 430eForth v4.3 in its complete source listing. The source code is commented liberally. However, in-line comments are only adequate to document the functions of the source code, but not sufficient for the intentions behind the source code. To give myself enough room to discuss the structures and the design requirements of all the commands, for one section of source code, I add another section of comments. I hope this format will let me explain more fully what the commands do and what was intended for them to do.

msp430g2553.h contains all the register names and names of bits in these registers. It is included here first so that I can refer to the registers and bits in standard MSP430 mnemonic names.

```
;;;;;;;;;;;;;;;;;;;;;;;;;;;;;;;;;;;;;;;;;;;;;;;;;;;;;;;;;;;;

        .nolist
        .title "msp430 eForth 4.3"
        .cdecls C,LIST,"msp430g2553.h"   ; Include device header file

;;;;;;;;;;;;;;;;;;;;;;;;;;;;;;;;;;;;;;;;;;;;;;;;;;;;;;;;;;;;
;
; 7/7/2012 430eForth1.0, from eForth86.asm and 430uForth
; 7/4/2012 Move 430uForth2.1 from IAR to CCS 5.2
; 8/5/2014 Move 430eForth2.2 to CCS 6.0.  Fix linkage of OVER.
;       Software UART at 2400 baud.
; 8/10/2014 430eForth2.3 9600 baud, thanks
; to Dirk Bruehl and Michael Kalus of www.4e4th.org
; 8/10/2014 430eForth2.4 Restore ERASE and WRITE
; 8/20/2014 430eForth2.5 Test Segment D
; 8/25/2014 430eForth2.6 Turnkey
; 8/26/2014 430eForth2.7 Optimize
; 9/16/2014 430eForth3.1 Tail recursion, APP!
; 10/11/2014 430eForth4.1 Direct thread, more optimization
```

```
; 10/23/2014 430eForth4.2 Direct thread, pack lists
; 11/12/2014 430eForth4.2 Direct thread, final

; Build for and verified on MSP430G2 LaunchPad from TI
; Assembled with Code Composer Sudio 6.0 IDE
; Internal DCO at 8 MHz
; Hardware UART at 9600 baud. TXD and RXD must be crossed.
;
```

4.1 Forth Virtual Machine

In the original eForth Model, Bill Muench identified 31 primitive commands in the kernel. These commands were coded in machine instructions of the host microprocessor. They allow the underlying microcontroller to become a Forth Virtual Machine. All other commands were written as compound commands, containing lists of tokens which specify execution behavior of commands. Compound commands are token lists of primitive commands and other compound commands. This division of primitive and compound commands was very useful in porting eForth to many different microprocessors, because only primitive commands needed to be rewritten when moving eForth to a new microcontroller.

In 430eForth v4.3, I retained this division. However, I tried optimize as many compound commands as possible, so that the system executes at the highest speed and occupies the least memory space. All commands that can be optimized are re-coded in assembly.

MSP430G2 is a 16-bit CPU with 16 16-bit registers. The CPU registers R4-R6 are assigned specific functions required in a Forth Virtual Machine as follows:

Register	FVM Name	Function
R0(PC)		Program counter
R1(SP)		Return stack pointer
R2(SR)		Status register
R3		Constant generator
R4	tos	Top of parameter stack
R5	stack	Parameter stack pointer
R6	ip	Interpretive pointer
R7	temp0	Scratch pad
R8	temp1	Scratch pad

R9	temp2	Scratch pad
R10	temp3	Scratch pad
R11		Not used
R12		Not used
R13		Not used
R14		Not used
R15		Not used

```
;;;;;;;;;;;;;;;;;;;;;;;;;;;;;;;;;;;;;;;;;;;;;;;;;;;;;;;;;;;;;;
;
; Direct Thread Model of eForth

;;      CPU registers
tos     .equ    R4
stack   .equ    R5
ip      .equ    R6
temp0   .equ    R7
temp1   .equ    R8
temp2   .equ    R9
temp3   .equ    R10
```

The Forth Virtual Machine as envisioned by 430eForth v4.3, hosted on MSP430G2, can be shown schematically in the following figure. Here the parameter stack and the return stack can be combined as a giant shift register group, 16 bit wide throughout. Top of stack register tos sits in between. All arithmetic and logic operations take one argument from tos, and an optional argument from top of parameter stack.

Top element on the return stack exchanges execution addresses with the ip register. The ip register sends execution address to pc register for execution. From this figure, I hope you get a clearer picture of a Forth Virtual Machine. This mythical Forth Virtual Machine was actually implemented in hardware in my eP32 microcontroller design. This is where hardware design blurs into software design. They express the same logic.

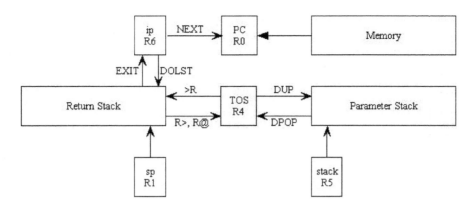

Assembly Macros

Assembly macros are pseudo machine instructions which assemble machine instruction sequences to simplify assembly programming. The original eForth Model was written for the 8086 processor, using MASM, the Macro Assembler from Microsoft, released with MSDOS in the 1980's. MASM was clean and efficient, and the source code of 86eForth.asm was very concise and very pleasing. When I ported eForth to other processors and used other so called 'Macro Assemblers', none of them could reproduce what MASM did.

Only the simplest macros worked consistently. None of them could handle string arguments like MASM. Most of them could not handle assembly variable consistently like MASM. In my utter frustration and disappointment, I decided to hand code the link field and name fields of all Forth command, leaving no chance for the assemblers to mess up my Forth dictionary structure. I figured that I had to do it only once, and I could use the same dictionary structure for all my later eForth implementations.

In 430eForth v4.3, I defined only 5 simple macros, doing straightforward replacement. They are useful in reminding me the basic parameter stack operations, and the inner interpreters of Forth Virtual Machine in handling primitive commands, and token lists of compound commands.

Pops	Pop the external parameter stack and copy the popped item into tos register. It is used to implement DROP commands, and many other commands consuming the top items on the parameter stack. It uses stack register in post-increment addressing mode

Pushs	Push the top item on the parameter stack, which is cached in tos register, on the external parameter stack. It is used to implement DUP command, and commands which push new data onto the parameter stack. It is slightly more complicated, because the MSP430 does not a have pre-decrement addressing mode.
$NEXT	This macro terminates all primitive commands. It copies the execution address pointed to by the ip register into the pc register, jumping to the execution address and starting executing a new command. It executes the next command in a list, hence the name $NEXT. Since the ip register is incremented automatically, pointing to the next execution address in the token list, at the end of the current command, $NEXT will continue 'interpreting' the token list.
$NEST	$NEST assembles a call #DOLST instruction at the beginning of every compound command, before the token list of execution addresses. The subroutine DOLST exchanges contents in the ip registers, with the top element on the return stack, pointed to by the sp register. It thus saves the current ip register on the return stack for the unfinished list to be returned to later, and points ip to the token list in the new compound command to scan and execute. At the end of this new list, there must be a command EXIT, which unnests the current command, and returns to the unfinished list, whose ip was saved on the return stack.
$CONST	$CONST assembles a call #DOCON instruction at the beginning of every constant or variable command, before the value of a constant, or a pointer to a RAM location for a variable, respectively. The subroutine DOCON fetches the contents of the next memory location in ROM memory and pushes the value on the parameter stack. Constant command gets a value, and variable command get a RAM pointer. They have the identical structures in the ROM memory.

```
;; Macros

pops    .macro ;DROP
        mov.w  @stack+,tos
        .endm

pushs   .macro ;DUP
```

```
        decd.w stack
        mov.w  tos,0(stack)
        .endm;; Constants

$NEXT   .macro
        mov @ip+,pc   ; fetch code address into PC
        .endm

$NEST   .macro
        .align 2
        call   #DOLST ; fetch code address into PC, W=PFA
        .endm

$CONST .macro
        .align 2
        call   #DOCON ; fetch code address into PC, W=PFA
        .endm
```

Constants Used by Assembler

MSP430G2553 is a small microcontroller, with 16 KB of flash memory and 512 B of RAM memory. I prefer lots of RAM, because Forth is an extensible language, and I can extend its dictionary more naturally in RAM. Nevertheless, 16 KB of flash memory is much better than the 2 KB of flash memory in the earlier MSP430G2213 on LaunchPad, which just could not host a reasonable Forth Virtual Machine. Memory allocation is severely restricted by the memory architecture. However, with enough memory resources, a Forth Virtual Machine can always adapt to its environment.

The memory map of 430eForth v4.3 as hosted on MSP430G2553 is shown in following figure:

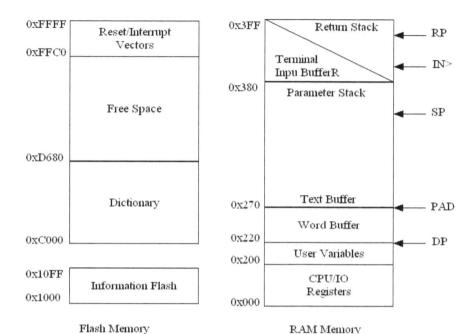

Flash Memory   RAM Memory

Constant	Value	Function
COMPO	$40	Lexicon compile-only bit
IMEDD	$80	Lexicon immediate bit
CELLL	2	Size of a cell in bytes
BASEE	10	Default radix for number conversion
BKSPP	8	Back space ASCII character
LF	10	Line feed ASCII character
CRR	13	Carriage return ASCII character
CALLL	$12B0	Machine code of call instruction
UPP	$200	Start of user area
DPP	$220	Start of free RAM space
SPP	$378	Top of parameter stack (SP0)
TIBB	$380	Terminal input buffer (TIB)
RPP	$3F8	Top of return stack (RP0)
CODEE	$C000	Start of Forth dictionary
COLDD	$FFFE	Reset vector
EM	$FFFF	Top of flash main memory

Flash memory allocation of 430eForth in bytes:

Address	Contents
$1000	Information flash memory, Segment D, for user variables
$C000	Start of Forth dictionary
$FFFE	End of Forth dictionary
$FFFF	End of flash memory

RAM memory allocation of 430eForth in bytes:

Address	Contents
$0	Special function and I/O registers
$200	User variables
$220	Free RAM space
$270	Initial PAD for number conversions
$378	Top of parameter stack
$380	Terminal input buffer
$3F8	Top of return stack

```
;; Assembler constants

COMPO   .equ    040H    ;lexicon compile only bit
IMEDD   .equ    080H    ;lexicon immediate bit
MASKK   .equ    07F1FH  ;lexicon bit mask
CELLL   .equ    2       ;size of a cell
BASEE   .equ    10      ;default radix
VOCSS   .equ    8       ;depth of vocabulary stack
BKSPP   .equ    8       ;backspace
LF      .equ    10      ;line feed
CRR     .equ    13      ;carriage return
ERR     .equ    27      ;error escape
TIC     .equ    39      ;tick
CALLL   .equ    012B0H  ;NOP CALL opcodes

UPP     .equ    200H
DPP     .equ    220H
SPP     .equ    378H    ;data stack
```

```
TIBB    .equ    380H    ;terminal input buffer
RPP     .equ    3F8H    ;return stacl
CODEE   .equ    0C000H  ;code dictionary
COLDD   .equ    0FFFEH  ;cold start vector
EM      .equ    0FFFFH  ;top of memory
```

Startup Code

Flash memory location 0FFFEH is allocated for a reset vector. The reset vector contains an address pointing to the reset routine main. When MSP430G2553 boots up, it jumps to main and starts running. main first initializes the return stack pointer sp, the parameter stack pointer stack, and the top of stack tos. It uses the default internal clock DCOCLK at about 1.1 MHz, until it is later configured to run at 8 MHz accurately to support a USART COM port. The watchdog timer is turned off. Two LED's on LaunchPad are turned on by initialized the P1DIR register in the GPIO port P1.

It then jumps to the eForth cold boot routine COLD, which starts the Forth text interpreter to execute commands you type in on a terminal emulator.

```
;;;;;;;;;;;;;;;;;;;;;;;;;;;;;;;;;;;;;;;;;;;;;;;;;;;;;;;;
        .list
;; Main entry points and COLD start data

        .text
        .global     main
main:
init:
        mov     #RPP,SP         ; set up stack
        mov     #SPP,stack
        clr     tos
        mov.w   #WDTPW+WDTHOLD,&WDTCTL   ; Stop watchdog timer
        bis.b   #041h,&P1DIR        ; P1.0/6 output
        jmp     COLD


;;;;;;;;;;;;;;;;;;;;;;;;;;;;;;;;;;;;;;;;;;;;;;;;;;;;;;;;
```

COLD is the last command defined in 430eForth_9.asm file. However, it brings up the Forth system, and this whole document is trying to explain it fully, following the source code. Here is a schematic drawing of the contents of COLD. It is enclosed in a big box, which contains a smaller box QUIT, which contains yet some smaller boxes. These boxes are Forth commands I will discuss later in details.

There are also many diamond boxes representing branch conditions. In the middle of the diagram there are two boxes $INTERPRET and $COMPILE. They are the text interpreter and command compiler. This is the best graphical representation of the eForth system I can give you. You have a bird's eye view of eForth to guide you through the following sections in minute details on how this system is constructed. You see the forest first. Later, you will see trees, flowers, and perhaps weeds. They are all essential parts of a living ecosystem.

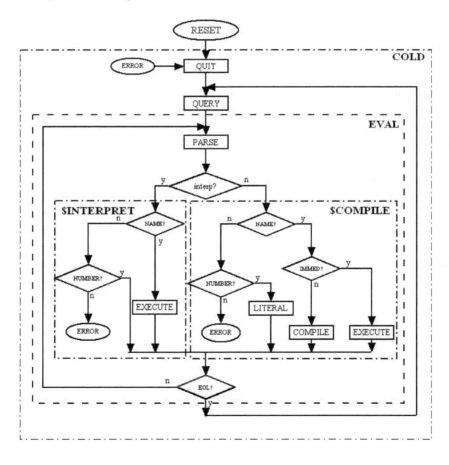

Since I am on the subject of COLD, I might just well show you the actual code of COLD. It first initializes the I/O registers with STOIO. Then it copies the user variables from Information Flash Memory Segment D at 0x1000 to RAM at 0x0200. Then it executes HI to send out eForth sign-on message to a terminal. Finally, it falls into the text interpreter QUIT. Now, Forth is running and you can communicate with it through the terminal.

```
;      COLD        ( -- )
;          The hilevel cold start sequence.
           .word  APPST-6
           .byte  4,"COLD",0
COLD
           $NEST
           .word  STOIO
           .word  DOLIT,UZERO,DOLIT,UPP
           .word  DOLIT,ULAST-UZERO,CMOVE      ;initialize user area
           .word  TBOOT,ATEXE   ;application boot
           .word  QUIT   ;start interpretation
```

Device Dependent I/O

The only I/O device 430eForth v4.3 needs is a USART COM port. To get this port running and communicate with a terminal emulator on PC, many other devices in MSP430G2553 have to be initialized properly. Once properly initialized, eForth will receive characters typed on a keyboard by the command KEY, and send characters to a terminal by the command EMIT.

MSP430G2553 on the LaunchPad does not have an external clock. It runs on an internal digitally controlled clock DCOCLK. This clock is calibrated to run accurately at 8 MHz to generate baud rate clocks for a USART. The DCO clock, the USART, and the P1 GPIO port driving the on board LED are initialized in the command STOIO, called by COLD, the startup command.

These are the only devices in MSP430G2 which have to be initialized to get Forth running. All other devices have to be initialized if you intend to use them in your application.

All interrupts are turned off. Interrupt is a big topic we do not want to deal with here. However, after you get your Forth running, it is not very difficult to add interrupt service routines and then turn on corresponding interrupts.

If you watch closely, each command starts with two lines of comments. One line with the name of the command, and its stack effects in parentheses. The next line comments on its function. After the comments, one .word instruction assembles a link field, and one .byte instruction assembles a name field. These two lines build a header of the command. In 430eForth v4.3, I removed the headers of many commands which I think will never be used by you in routine programming.

Only 125 commands retain their headers and can be used to compose new compound commands. This way the Forth programming language is greatly simplified for casual programmers to build useful applications easily. If you are a serious Forth programmer and need all the commands offered by 430eForth v4.3, you can un-comment the headers. But, do be careful with the link fields to maintain the linking chain of all the command records in this system.

A label right after the name field identifies the execution address of this command. This label will be referenced as tokens in later lists of execution addresses in other compound command. In the assembly source, we have the actual name of a command, which is exposed to you, and the label of a command, which is known to the assembler only. When I will talk about a command whose name is hidden, I will refer to it by its label, to make it easier to find in the source listing.

A name field contains a length byte and a character string, which is the actual name of the command. Names are restricted to 31 characters, and only the least significant 5 bits are used for length. Bit 5 in length byte is called 'Immediate' bit and bit 6 is called 'Compile-Only' bit. Commands with immediate bit set are Immediate Commands, and they are executed rather compiled when the text interpreter is in compiling mode. Commands with the Compile-Only bit set can only be compiled and cannot be interpreted. Compile-Only commands would generally crash the Forth system if allowed to be executed interactively.

The name field is null-filled to the 2 byte word boundary, so that the following code field always begins on an even word boundary. The link field also begins on an even word boundary.

The following figure shows the structure of a Forth command, with a link field, a name field, and a code filed.

Link Field	

Name Field	ASCII	O/C/I/Length
	ASCII	ASCII
	0	ASCII

Code Field

Structure of eForth Commands

?KEY	If RXBUF register received a character, push the character on stack, and a true flag on top of the character. Push a false flag if RXBUF register is empty.
KEY	Wait until a character is received in the RXBUF register of USART0. The ASCII code of the received character is pushed on parameter stack.
EMIT	Transmit a character in tos to TXBUF of USART.
STOIO	Initialize DCOCLK, USART0, and P1 I/O port.

```
;; Device dependent I/O

;    ?KEY      ( -- F | c T )
;       Return input character.
         .word  0
         .byte  4,"?KEY",0
```

```
QKEY:
      pushs
QKEY1:
      BIT.B   #UCA0RXIFG,&IFG2
      JZ      FALSE   ;return false flag
      MOV.B   &UCA0RXBUF,tos      ; read character into TOS
      pushs
      jmp     TRUE

;   KEY       ( -- c )
;       Return input character.
      .word   QKEY-6
      .byte   3,"KEY"
KEY
      pushs
KEY1:
      BIT.B   #UCA0RXIFG,&IFG2
      JZ      KEY1
      MOV.B   &UCA0RXBUF,tos      ; read character into TOS
      $NEXT

;   EMIT      ( c -- )
;       Send character c to the output device.
      .word   KEY-4
      .byte   4,"EMIT",0
EMIT
EMIT1:
      BIT.B   #UCA0TXIFG,&IFG2
      JZ      EMIT1
      MOV.B   tos,&UCA0TXBUF
      pops
      $NEXT

;   !IO       ( -- )
;       Initialize the serial I/O devices.
;       .word   EMIT-6
;       .byte   3,"!IO"
STOIO
; 8MHz
```

```
        mov.b    &CALBC1_8MHZ, &BCSCTL1     ; Set DCO
        mov.b    &CALDCO_8MHZ, &DCOCTL      ; to 8 MHz.
        mov.b    #006h, &P1SEL       ; Use P1.1/P1.2 for USCI_A0
        mov.b    #006h, &P1SEL2      ; Use P1.1/P1.2 for USCI_A0
; Configure UART (Koch)
        bis.b    #UCSSEL_2,&UCA0CTL1        ;db2 SMCLK
        mov.b    #65,&UCA0BR0        ;db3 8MHz 9600 Insgesamt &833
= $341
        mov.b    #3,&UCA0BR1 ;db4 8MHz 9600
        mov.b    #UCBRS_2,&UCA0MCTL ;db5 Modulation UCBRSx = 2
        bic.b    #UCSWRST,&UCA0CTL1 ;db6 **Initialize USCI
        $NEXT    ;called from COLD
```

4.2 Kernel

The kernel is a minimal collection of primitive Forth commands which must be coded in the native machine instructions to get a Forth Virtual Machine to run. From this set of primitive commands, you can build a large set of compound commands, which contain token lists of execution addresses of primitive and compound commands. A Forth Virtual Machine must be able to run, or process, both types of commands. In 430eForth v4.3, I implemented constants and variables as a separated type of commands for efficiency. These three types of commands are illustrated in the following figure:

Primitive Command

Machine Instructions	$NEXT

Compound Command

call DOLST	Token List of Execution Addresses	EXIT

Constant Command

call DOCON	Value

Variable Command

call DOCON	Pointer to RAM

Create Array Command

call DOCON	Pointer to RAM

Inner Interpreter

Primitive commands contain sequences of machine instructions, which are executed by CPU. Primitive commands are terminated by a macro instruction $NEXT, which automatically jumps to the next command in the current token list of execution addresses. The interpret pointer ip is in register R6, pointing to the token to be executed next.

Compound commands must start with a macro instruction $NEST, which assembles a call #DOLST machine instruction. DOLST saves the ip register from the previous token list to the return stack, and uses the ip register to scan a new or current token list. At the end of the current token list, there must be a token EXIT, which retrieves the ip saved on the return stack and continue on the unfinished portion of the previous token list.

$NEXT uses ip to scan a token list. $NEST allows token lists to be nested. EXIT unnests one list. Compound commands are nested like a tree with branches on branches. At the end of a terminal branch, there must be a leaf of a primitive command to terminate the nesting, and begin the unnesting process. Nesting and unnesting of token lists are shown in the following figure:

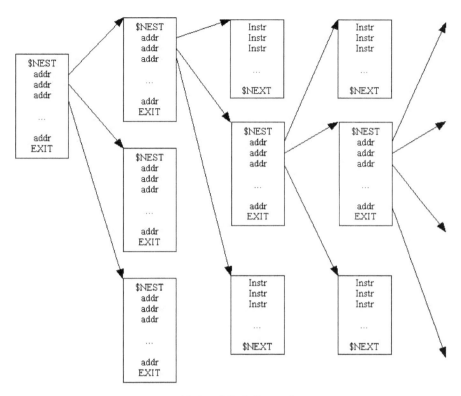

Nesting of eForth Commands

Constant commands and variable commands have identical structures in this 430eForth v4.3 implementation. These commands are stored in flash memory, and there is no problem storing a constant value in the flash memory. However, variables have to be stored in RAM memory so that they can be changed. In the variable command record, we store a memory pointer to a location in RAM memory, and the contents in this RAM memory can be changed at will.

A macro instruction $CONST is used to construct constant and variable commands. $CONST assembles a machine instruction call #DOCON, follow by a constant value or a RAM memory pointer. The subroutine DOCON simply pushes this value or pointer on the parameter stack.

DOLIT	Start an integer literal structure in a compound command. It allows numbers to be pushed onto the parameter stack at run time when the compound command is executed.
DOCON	Start a constant or a variable command. It pushes the following value assembled in flash memory on the parameter stack.
DOLST	Start a compound command. It exchanges ip registers with the top element on the return stack, which happens to be the beginning of the token list in this compound command.
EXECUTE	Jump to an execution address on the top of the parameter stack. You cannot jump through the tos register directly, because this address has to be popped off the stack first.
EXIT	Terminate a compound command. The previous ip saved on return stack is popped back into ip register. Current command is terminated, and the previous command interrupted by the current command will continue. EXIT un-nests what $NEST did, and thus allows compound commands to nest and un-nest indefinitely.
@EXECUTE	Fetch an execution address of a command which is stored in the address on the top of the parameter stack, and executes this command. It is used to execute vectored commands stored in RAM memory. The behavior of a vectored command can be changed dynamically at the run time.

$NEXT, $NEST, and EXIT are the inner interpreters in eForth. They get commands executed continually. The inner interpreter is not a central program which executes commands in sequence. The Forth inner interpreters are distributed to all commands, in that each command knows how to pull out the next command and executes it. However, an execution sequence must start somehow, somewhere. EXECUT and @EXECUTE are the commands you can start executing a new command, if you know where that command is located, i.e., its execution address.

DOLIT starts an integer literal structure in a token list. A token list is a list of execution addresses. You cannot insert an integer into the token list, because it will get executed, and generally would crash the system. An integer literal begins with DOLIT, followed by the integer. When DOLIT is executed, it pushes the following integer on the parameter stack, and increment the ip register to skip over the integer.

```
;; The kernel

;   doLIT      ( -- w )
;       Push an inline literal.
;       .word  STOIO-4
;       .byte  COMPO+5,"doLIT"
DOLIT:
        pushs
        mov    @ip+,tos
        $NEXT

;   doCON      ( -- a )
;       Run time routine for CONSTANT, VARIABLE and CREATE.
;       .word  DOLIT-6
;       .byte  COMPO+5,"doCON"
DOCON:
        pushs
        pop    tos
        mov    @tos,tos
        $NEXT

;   doLIST     ( -- )
;       Process colon list..
;       .word  EMIT-6
;       .byte  6,"doLIST",0
DOLST
        mov    ip,temp0      ;exchange pointers
        pop    ip     ;push return stack
        push   temp0  ;restore the pointers
        $NEXT

;   EXIT       ( -- )
;       Terminate a colon definition.
        .word  EMIT-6
        .byte  4,"EXIT",0
EXIT
        mov    @sp+,ip
        $NEXT
```

```
;    EXECUTE    ( ca -- )
;        Execute the word at ca.
         .word  EXIT-6
         .byte  7,"EXECUTE"
EXECU
         mov    tos,temp0
         pops
         br     temp0


;    @EXECUTE   ( a -- )
;        Execute vector stored in address a.
         .word  EXECU-8
         .byte  8,"@EXECUTE",0
ATEXE
         mov    @tos,temp0
         pops
         br     temp0
```

Flow Control

Compound commands contain linear lists of tokens, which are execution addresses in 430eForth v4.3. Normally, the tokens are executed in a liner sequence. However, processing power of token lists of is greatly enhanced if we can change the execution sequence dynamically at run time. We can now extend the concept of tokens to structures of tokens. A structure is a tokens list, which has only one entry point and one exit point, but has branches and loops in between.

Therefore, structures can be string together linearly, just like tokens. Inside a structure, tokens can be arranged in branches, and in loops. Execution sequence can change dynamically among the branches and loops, depending upon run time conditions. Branches and loops must not extend beyond a structure, so that structures can still be strung together linearly. This is the principle of Structural Programming. Over the years, we had been reassured that all computable problems could be solved with structural programming. Forth embodied this principle explicitly, even before structural programming was first invented by Edsger Dijkstra in 1968.

BRAN, QBRAN, and DONXT are used to build branch and loop structures. However, microscopically, they are address literals similar to the integer literal with DOLIT. They are commands followed by addresses instead of integers. When they are executed at run time, the interpret pointer ip points to the address cell. This address may be copied into ip register, and causing a branch to that address and changing the execution sequence in a structure.

BRAN branches unconditionally. QBRAN does the branch when tos is zero. They are used to construct IF-ELSE-THEN, BEGIN-AGAIN, BEGIN-UNTIL, and BEGIN-WHILE-REPEAT structures. DONXT is used to build FOR-NEXT loop structure.

BRAN is compiled by AFT, ELSE, REPEAT and AGAIN. QBRAN is compiled by IF, WHILE and UNTIL. DONXT is compiled by NEXT. The integer literal and address literals are shown in the next figure.

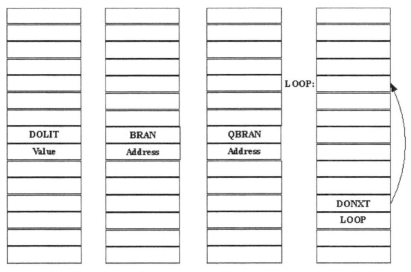

Integer Literal   BRAN Address Literal   QBRAN Address Literal   DONXT Address Literal

QBRAN	Start a conditional branch in a compound command.
BRAN	Start an unconditional branch in a compound command.
DONXT	Terminate an indexed loop in a compound command. A loop starts when the loop index is pushed on the return stack by FOR. When DONXT is executed, it decrements this loop index on the return stack. If the resulting index is not negative, jump back to repeat the loop. If the resulting index is negative, discard the index, increment ip and exit the loop.

```
;    branch    ( -- )
;        Branch to an inline address.
;        .word  ATEXE-10
;        .byte  COMPO+6,"branch",0
BRAN
         mov    @ip+,ip
         $NEXT


;    ?branch   ( f -- )
;        Branch if flag is zero.
;        .word  BRAN-8
;        .byte  COMPO+7,"?branch"
QBRAN
         tst    tos
         pops
         jz     BRAN
         jmp    SKIP


;    next      ( -- )
;        Run time code for the single index loop.
;        : next ( -- ) \ hilevel model
;        r> r> dup if 1 - >r @ >r exit then drop cell+ >r ;
;        .word  QBRAB-8
;        .byte  COMPO+4,"next",0
DONXT
         dec    0(sp)    ;decrement index
         jge    BRAN     ;loop back
         incd.w sp       ;discard index
SKIP:
         incd.w ip       ;exit loop
         $NEXT
```

Memory Access

MSP430G2553 has RAM memory and flash memory in different regions of the memory map. The same set of memory read commands can be used to read either RAM or flash memory. However, a different set of commands is necessary to write to flash memory. The flash memory writing commands will be discussed later with the command compiler in Section 4.4.

@	Read a 16-bit data stored in the address on top of the parameter stack. The address is a byte address pointing to a location in memory.
!	Store the 16-bit data as the second item on parameter stack into the address on top of the parameter stack.
C@	Read an 8-bit data stored in the address on top of the parameter stack.
C!	Store an 8-bit data as the second item on parameter stack into the address on top of the parameter stack.

The read memory commands read data stored in RAM and ROM memory. The write commands write only into the RAM memory. Since in MSP430G2553, the I/O registers are also mapped to the RAM memory space from 0 to $1FF, we can control MSP430G2553 interactively using these commands. This is the greatest advantage 430eForth has over the C/C++ programming environment which is a Compile-Load-Test non-interactive system.

To write to flash memory, we have the I!, ERASE, and WRITE commands. They will be discussed in Section 4.4 on command compiler.

```
;    !  ( w a -- )
;        Pop the data stack to memory.
        .word  ATEXE-10
        .byte  1,"!"
STORE
        mov.w  @stack+,0(tos)
        pops
        $NEXT


;    @  ( a -- w )
;        Push memory location to the data stack.
        .word  STORE-2
        .byte  1,"@"
AT
        mov.w  @tos,tos
        $NEXT


;    C! ( c b -- )
;        Pop the data stack to byte memory.
        .word  AT-2
```

```
        .byte  2,"C!",0
CSTOR
        mov.b  @stack+,0(tos)
        inc    stack
        pops
        $NEXT


;   C@ ( b -- c )
;       Push byte memory location to the data stack.
        .word  CSTOR-4
        .byte  2,"C@",0
CAT
        mov.b  @tos,tos
        $NEXT
```

Return Stack

430eForth system uses the return stack for two specific purposes: to save ip addresses while recursing through nested token lists, and to store the loop index for a FOR-NEXT loop.

Return stack is used by the Forth Virtual Machine to save return addresses to be processed later. It is also a convenient place to store data temporarily. The return stack can thus be considered as an extension of the parameter stack. However, you must be very careful in using the return stack for temporary storage. The data pushed on the return stack must be popped off before EXIT is executed. Otherwise, EXIT will get the wrong address to return to, and the system generally will crash. Since manipulating the return stack with >R and R> commands are very dangerous, they are designated as Compile-Only commands and you can only use them in the compiling mode.

In setting up a loop, FOR compiles >R, which pushes the loop index from the parameter stack to the return stack. Inside the FOR-NEXT loop, the running index can be recalled by R@. NEXT compiles DONXT with an address after FOR. When DONXT is executed, it decrements the loop index on the top of the return stack. If the index becomes negative, the loop is terminated by incrementing ip over the address; otherwise, DONXT branches back to the command after FOR.

RPSTO	Initialize return stack pointer.
>R	Pop a number off the parameter stack and pushes it on the return stack.
R>	Pop a number off the return stack and pushes it on the parameter stack.
R@	Copy the top item on the return stack and pushes it on the parameter stack without disturbing the return stack

```
;    RP!        ( -- )
;       init return stack pointer.
;       .word  CAT-4
;       .byte  3,"RP!"
RPSTO:
        mov    #RPP,SP       ;init return stack
        $NEXT


;    R> ( -- w )
;       Pop the return stack to the data stack.
        .word  CAT-4
        .byte  2,"R",3EH,0
RFROM
        pushs
        pop    tos
        $NEXT


;    R@ ( -- w )
;       Copy top of return stack to the data stack.
        .word  RFROM-4
        .byte  2,"R@",0
RAT
        pushs
        mov    0(sp),tos
        $NEXT


;    >R ( w -- )
;       Push the data stack to the return stack.
        .word  RAT-4
        .byte  COMPO+2,">R",0
TOR
        push   tos
        pops
        $NEXT
```

Parameter Stack

The parameter stack is the central location where all numerical data are processed, and where parameters are passed from one command to another. The stack items have to be arranged properly so that they can be retrieved in the Last-In-First-Out (LIFO) manner. When stack items are out of order, they can be rearranged by the stack commands DUP, SWAP, OVER and DROP. There are other stack commands useful in manipulating stack items, but these four are considered to be the classic stack commands.

In 430eForth v4.3, the parameter stack pointer is called stack, and it uses R5 register. Top element of the parameter stack is cached in R4 register, called tos. The second element which is on the actual stack in RAM can be referenced by various addressing modes as @stack, @stack+, and 0(stack), depending on actual usage.

SPSTO	Initialize parameter stack pointer and tos.
SP@	Push the current parameter stack pointer on top of parameter stack. It is used to determine the depth of parameter stack.
DROP	Pop the parameter stack, and discards the top item on it.
DUP	Duplicate the top item and pushes it on the parameter stack.
SWAP	Exchange two top items on the parameter stack.
OVER	Duplicates the second item and pushes it on the parameter stack.

```
;    SP!          ( -- )
;        Init data stack pointer.
;        .word  SPAT-4
;        .byte  3,"SP!"
SPSTO:
        mov    #SPP,stack    ;init parameter stack
        clr    tos
        $NEXT

;    DROP         ( w -- )
;        Discard top stack item.
        .word  TOR-4
        .byte  4,"DROP",0
DROP:
```

```
        pops
        $NEXT


;    DUP        ( w -- w w )
;        Duplicate the top stack item.
        .word  DROP-6
        .byte  3,"DUP"
DUPP:
        pushs
        $NEXT


;    SWAP       ( w1 w2 -- w2 w1 )
;        Exchange top two stack items.
        .word  DUPP-4
        .byte  4,"SWAP",0
SWAP
        mov.w  tos,temp0
        mov.w  @stack,tos
        mov.w  temp0,0(stack)
        $NEXT


;    OVER       ( w1 w2 -- w1 w2 w1 )
;        Copy second stack item to top.
        .word  SWAP-6
        .byte  4,"OVER",0
OVER:
        mov.w  @stack,temp0
        pushs
        mov.w  temp0,tos
        $NEXT
```

Logic and Maths

The only primitive command which cares about logic is QBRAN. It tests the top item on the stack. If it is zero, QBRAN will branch to the following address. If it is not zero, QBRAN will ignore the following address and execute the command after the branch address. Thus we distinguish two logic values, zero for false and non-zero for true. TRUE and FALSE are code endings which sets tos to -1 or clears tos to 0, respectively.

Numbers used this way are called logic flags which can be either true or false. Logic flags cause conditional branching in structures.

0<	Examine the top item on the parameter stack for its negativeness. If it is negative, return a –1 for true. If it is 0 or positive, return a 0 for false.
AND	Pop second item on the parameter stack and AND it to tos.
OR	Pop second item on the parameter stack and OR it to tos.
XOR	Pop second item on the parameter stack and XOR it to tos.
UM+	Add top two unsigned number on the data stack and replaces them with the unsigned sum of these two numbers and a carry in tos. Forth Virtual Machine does not have access to the carry flag in MSP430G2 CPU, and UM+ preserves the carry flag to be used in double integer arithmetic operations. In 430eForth v4.3, most arithmetic commands are coded in assembly and UM+ is not used often.

```
;    0< ( n -- t )
;        Return true if n is negative.
        .word   OVER-6
        .byte   2,"0",3CH,0
ZLESS:
        tst     tos
        jn      TRUE
FALSE:
        clr     tos
        $NEXT
TRUE:
        mov     #0x-1,tos
        $NEXT


;    AND         ( w w -- w )
;        Bitwise AND.
        .word   ZLESS-4
        .byte   3,"AND"
ANDD
        and     @stack+,tos
        $NEXT
```

```
;    OR ( w w -- w )
;        Bitwise inclusive OR.
         .word  ANDD-4
         .byte  2,"OR",0
ORR
         bis    @stack+,tos
         $NEXT


;    XOR       ( w w -- w )
;        Bitwise exclusive OR.
         .word  ORR-4
         .byte  3,"XOR"
XORR
         xor    @stack+,tos
         $NEXT


;    UM+       ( w w -- w cy )
;        Add two numbers, return the sum and carry flag.
         .word  XORR-4
         .byte  3,"UM+"
UPLUS
         add    @stack,tos
         mov    tos,0(stack)
         clr    tos
         rlc    tos
         $NEXT
```

Common Functions

These commands are commonly used in writing Forth applications. In the original eForth Model, they were coded as compound commands for portability. In 430eForth v4.3, they are mostly recoded in assembly for performance and to save memory. Most assembly code are fairly short, showing that MSP430G2 is a very good host for a Forth Virtual Machine.

?DUP	Duplicate the top item on the parameter stack if it is non-zero.
ROT	Rotate the top three items on the parameter stack. The third item is pulled out to the top. The second item is pushed down to the third item, and the top item is pushed down to be the second item. ROT is unique in that it accesses the third item on the parameter stack. All other stack commands can only access one or two stack items. In Forth programming, it is generally accepted that you should not try to access stack items deeper than the third item. When you have to access deeper into the data stack, it is a good time to re-evaluate your algorithm. Most often, you can avoid this situation by factoring your code into smaller parts which do not reach so deep into the parameter stack.
2DROP	Discard the top two items on the parameter stack.
2DUP	Duplicate the top two items on the parameter stack.
+	Pop the second item off stack and add it to the top item on the stack.
NOT	Invert each individual bit in the top item on the parameter stack. It is often called 1's complement operation.
NEGATE	Negate the top item on the parameter stack. It is often called 2's complement operation.
DNEGATE	Negate the top two items on the parameter stack, as a 32-bit double integer.
-	Subtract the top item on the parameter stack from the second item, and pop the top item off the parameter stack.
ABS	Replace the top item on the parameter stack with its absolute value.

```
;; Common functions

;    ?DUP      ( w -- w w | 0 )
;       Dup tos if its is not zero.
         .word  UPLUS-4
         .byte  4,"?DUP",0
QDUP
         tst    tos
         jnz    DUPP
         $NEXT
```

```
;    ROT       ( w1 w2 w3 -- w2 w3 w1 )
;       Rot 3rd item to top.
        .word  QDUP-6
        .byte  3,"ROT"
ROT
        mov.w  0(stack),temp0
        mov.w  tos,0(stack)
        mov.w  2(stack),tos
        mov.w  temp0,2(stack)
        $NEXT


;    2DROP     ( w w -- )
;       Discard two items on stack.
        .word  ROT-4
        .byte  5,"2DROP"
DDROP
        incd.w stack
        pops
        $NEXT


;    2DUP      ( w1 w2 -- w1 w2 w1 w2 )
;       Duplicate top two items.
        .word  DDROP-6
        .byte  4,"2DUP",0
DDUP
        mov.w  @stack,temp0
        pushs
        decd.w stack
        mov.w  temp0,0(stack)
        $NEXT


;    +  ( w w -- sum )
;       Add top two items.
        .word  DDUP-6
        .byte  1,"+"
PLUS
        add    @stack+,tos
        $NEXT
```

```
;   D+ ( d d -- d )
;       Double addition, as an example using UM+.
;
        .word  PLUS-2
        .byte  2,"D+",0
DPLUS
        mov.w  @stack+,temp0
        mov.w  @stack+,temp1
        add.w  temp0,0(stack)
        addc   temp1,tos
        $NEXT


;   NOT         ( w -- w )
;       One's complement of tos.
        .word  DPLUS-4
        .byte  3,"NOT"
INVER
        inv    tos
        $NEXT


;   NEGATE      ( n -- -n )
;       Two's complement of tos.
        .word  INVER-4
        .byte  6,"NEGATE",0
NEGAT
        inv    tos
        inc    tos
        $NEXT


;   DNEGATE     ( d -- -d )
;       Two's complement of top double.
        .word  NEGAT-8
        .byte  7,"DNEGATE"
DNEGA:
        inv    tos
        inv 0(stack)
        inc    0(stack)
        addc   #0,tos
        $NEXT
```

```
;   -   ( n1 n2 -- n1-n2 )
;       Subtraction.
        .word  DNEGA-8
        .byte  1,"-"
SUBB
        sub    @stack+,tos
        jmp    NEGAT


;   ABS        ( n -- n )
;       Return the absolute value of n.
        .word  SUBB-2
        .byte  3,"ABS"
ABSS
        tst.w  tos
        jn     NEGAT
        $NEXT
```

Comparisons

The primitive comparison commands in 430eForth are QBRAN and 0<. However, QBRAN is at such a low level that it is not used at all in compound commands. It is secretly compiled into compound commands by IF as an address literal. For all intentions and purposes, we can consider IF the equivalent of QBRAN. When IF is encountered, the top item on the parameter stack is considered a logic flag. If it is true (non-zero), the execution continues until ELSE, then jump to THEN, or to THEN directly if there is no ELSE clause.

Here are the other commonly used comparison commands.

=	Compare top two items on the parameter stack. If they are equal, replace these two items with a true flag; otherwise, replace them with a false flag.
U<	Compare two unsigned numbers on the top of the parameter stack. If the top item is less than the second item in unsigned comparison, replace these two items with a true flag; otherwise, replace them with a false flag. This command is very important, especially in comparing addresses, as we assume that the addresses are unsigned numbers pointing to unique memory locations. The arithmetic comparison

	operator < cannot be used to determine whether one address is higher or lower than the other. Using < for address comparison had been the single cause of many failures in the annals of Forth. This problem in MSP430G2553 is more significant since the flash memory is in the upper 32 KB of memory space.
<	Compare two signed numbers on the top of the parameter stack. If the second item is less than the top item in signed comparison, replace these two items with a true flag; otherwise, replace them with a false flag.
>	Compare two signed numbers on the top of the parameter stack. If the second item is greater than the top item in signed comparison, replace these two items with a true flag; otherwise, replace them with a false flag.
MAX	Retain the larger of the top two items on the parameter stack. Both numbers are assumed to be signed integers.
MIN	Retain the smaller of the top two items on the parameter stack. Both numbers are assumed to be signed integers.

```
;    =  ( w w -- t )
;       Return true if top two are equal.
        .word  ABSS-4
        .byte  1,3DH
EQUAL
        xor    @stack+,tos
        jnz    FALSE
        jmp    TRUE


;    U< ( u u -- t )
;       Unsigned compare of top two items.
        .word  EQUAL-2
        .byte  2,"U",3CH,0
ULESS
        mov    @stack+,temp0
        cmp    tos,temp0
        subc   tos,tos
        $NEXT
```

```
;   <  ( n1 n2 -- t )
;       Signed compare of top two items.
        .word  ULESS-4
        .byte  1,3CH
LESS
        cmp     @stack+,tos
        jz      FALSE
        jge     TRUE
        jmp     FALSE


;   >  ( n1 n2 -- t )
;       Signed compare of top two items.
        .word  LESS-2
        .byte  1,3EH
GREAT
        cmp     @stack+,tos
        jge     FALSE
        jmp     TRUE


;   MAX        ( n n -- n )
;       Return the greater of two top stack items.
        .word  GREAT-2
        .byte  3,"MAX"
MAX:
        cmp     0(stack),tos
MAX1:
        jl      DROP
        incd.w stack
        $NEXT


;   MIN        ( n n -- n )
;       Return the smaller of top two stack items.
        .word  MAX-4
        .byte  3,"MIN"
MIN:
        cmp     tos,0(stack)
        jmp     MAX1
```

Divide

UM/MOD and UM* are the most complicated and comprehensive division and multiplication commands. Once they are coded, all other division and multiplication operators can be derived easily from them. It has been a tradition in Forth programming since Chuck Moore that one solves the most difficult problem first, and all other problems are solved by themselves.

Chuck Moore introduce the multiply step and divide step machine instructions in MuP21. They were also implemented in my P-series of microcontrollers as machine instructions. They are not difficult to implement in other microcontrollers with 16-bit add and subtract instructions.

UM/MOD is coded in assembly. It repeats a divide step to produce a quotient and a remainder.

To divide a 32-bit unsigned double integer dividend by a 16-bit unsigned divisor, we first move the divisor from tos to register temp0. Then pop the stack so that the high half of the dividend is in tos, and the lower half of dividend is on the parameter stack. They form a 32-bit shift register. Compare tos with temp0. If temp0>=tos, subtract temp0 from tos, and shift the whole dividend left 1 bit, and set bit 0 in (stack) to 1. If temp0<tos, just shift the whole dividend left 1 bit, and clear bit 0 in (stack) to 0. Repeat this procedure 16 times, and you get the 2xquotient on stack and the remainder in tos.

The following figure will help you visualize this divide step operation.

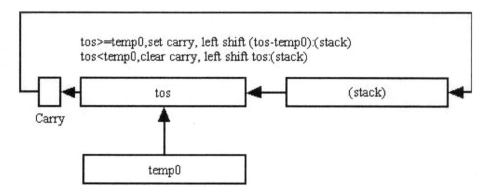

UM/MOD	Divide an unsigned double integer by an unsigned single integer. It returns the unsigned remainder and unsigned quotient on the parameter stack. It is coded in assembly. The divisor is popped to register temp0. The double integer dividend is on the stack. Division is carried out in steps similar to long hand division.
M/MOD	Divide a signed double integer by a signed single integer. It returns the signed remainder and signed quotient on the parameter stack.
/MOD	Divide a signed single integer by a signed integer. It replaces these two items with the signed remainder and quotient.
MOD	Divide a signed single integer by a signed integer. It replaces these two items with the signed remainder only.
/	Divide a signed single integer by a signed integer. It replaces these two items with the signed quotient only.

```
;; Divide

;    UM/MOD    ( udl udh u -- ur uq )
;        Unsigned divide of a double by a single. Return mod and
quotient.
        .word   MIN-4
        .byte   6,"UM/MOD",0
UMMOD:
        mov     tos,temp0
        pops
        mov     #17,temp1
UMMOD2:
        cmp     temp0,tos
        jnc     UMMOD3
        sub     temp0,tos
        setc
        jmp     UMMOD4
UMMOD3:
        clrc
UMMOD4:
        rlc     0(stack)
        rlc     tos
        dec     temp1
```

```
        jnz    UMMOD2
        rra    tos
        mov    tos,temp0
        mov    0(stack),tos
        mov    temp0,0(stack)
        $NEXT
```

```
;   M/MOD     ( d n -- r q )
;       Signed floored divide of double by single. Return mod and
quotient.
        .word  UMMOD-8
        .byte  5,"M/MOD"
MSMOD
        $NEST
        .word  DUPP,ZLESS,DUPP,TOR,QBRAN,MMOD1
        .word  NEGAT,TOR,DNEGA,RFROM
MMOD1:
        .word  TOR,DUPP,ZLESS,QBRAN,MMOD2
        .word  RAT,PLUS
MMOD2:
        .word  RFROM,UMMOD,RFROM,QBRAN,MMOD3
        .word  SWAP,NEGAT,SWAP
MMOD3:
        .word  EXIT
```

```
;   /MOD      ( n n -- r q )
;       Signed divide. Return mod and quotient.
        .word  MSMOD-6
        .byte  4,"/MOD",0
SLMOD
        $NEST
        .word  OVER,ZLESS,SWAP,MSMOD,EXIT
```

```
;   MOD       ( n n -- r )
;       Signed divide. Return mod only.
        .word  SLMOD-6
        .byte  3,"MOD"
MODD
        $NEST
```

```
        .word   SLMOD,DROP,EXIT

;   /   ( n n -- q )
;       Signed divide. Return quotient only.
        .word   MODD-4
        .byte   1,"/"
SLASH
        $NEST
        .word   SLMOD,SWAP,DROP,EXIT
```

Multiply

UM* is recoded in assembly. It repeats the following multiply steps 16 times to build a 32-bit product.

To multiply a 16-bit unsigned integer multiplicand by a 16-bit unsigned multiplier, we first clear register temp0 as the higher half of the product. The multiplicand is in tos and the multiplier is on the parameter stack as 0(stack), which will become the lower half of the product. temp0 and 0(stack) form a 32-bit shift register. If bit 0 of 0(stack) is set, add tos to temp0, and shift the whole product right 1 bit, and the carry is shifted to bit 15 in temp0. If bit 0 of 0(stack) is cleared, just shift the whole product right 1 bit, and a 0 is shifted to bit 15 in temp0. Repeat this procedure 16 times, and you get the higher half of product in temp0 and the lower half in 0(stack).

The following figure will help you visualize this multiply step operation.

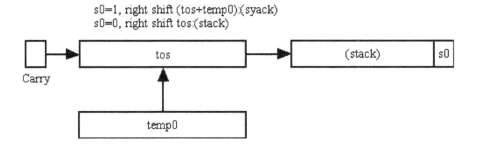

UM*	Multiply two unsigned single integers and returns the unsigned double integer product on the parameter stack. UM* is coded in assembly as discussed above.
*	Multiply two signed single integers and returns the signed single integer product on the parameter stack.
M*	Multiply two signed single integers and returns the signed double integer product on the parameter stack.
*/MOD	Multiply the signed integers n1 and n2, and then divides the double integer product by n3. It in fact is ratioing n1 by n2/n3. It returns both the remainder and the quotient.
*/	Multiply the signed integers n1 and n2, and then divides the double integer product by n3. It returns only the quotient.

Forth is very close to assembly languages in that it generally only handles integer numbers. There are floating point extensions in more sophisticated Forth systems, but they are more exceptions than rules. The reason why Forth has traditionally been an integer language is that integers are handled faster and more efficiently by the computers, and most technical problems can be solved satisfactorily using only integers.

A 16-bit integer has the dynamic range of 110 dB which is far more than enough for most engineering problems. The precision of a 16-bit integer representation is limited to one part in 65535, which could be inadequate for small numbers. However, the precision can be greatly improved by scaling; i.e., taking the ratio of two integers. It was demonstrated that pi, or any other irrational numbers, can be represented accurately to 1 part in 100,000,000 by a ratio of two 16-bit integers.

The scaling commands */MOD and */ are useful in scaling number n1 by the ratio of n2/n3. When n2 and n3 are properly chosen, the scaling commands can preserve precision similar to the floating point operations at a much higher speed. Notice also that in these scaling operations, the intermediate product of n1 and n2 is a double precision integer so that the precision of scaling is maintained.

```
;; Multiply

;    UM*         ( u u -- ud )
;        Unsigned multiply. Return double product.
         .word  SLASH-2
```

```
        .byte  3,"UM*"
UMSTA:
        clr    temp0
        mov    #16,temp1
UMSTA2:
        bit    #1,0(stack)
        jz     UMSTA3
        add    tos,temp0
        jmp    UMSTA4
UMSTA3:
        clrc
UMSTA4:
        rrc    temp0
        rrc    0(stack)
        dec    temp1
        jnz    UMSTA2
        mov    temp0,tos
        $NEXT


;    *  ( n n -- n )
;       Signed multiply. Return single product.
        .word  UMSTA-4
        .byte  1,"*"
STAR
        $NEST
        .word  UMSTA,DROP,EXIT


;    M* ( n n -- d )
;       Signed multiply. Return double product.
        .word  STAR-2
        .byte  2,"M*",0
MSTAR
        $NEST
        .word  DDUP,XORR,ZLESS,TOR
        .word  ABSS,SWAP,ABSS,UMSTA,RFROM
        .word  QBRAN,MSTA1
        .word  DNEGA
MSTA1:
        .word  EXIT
```

```
;    */MOD     ( n1 n2 n3 -- r q )
;       Multiply n1 and n2, then divide by n3. Return mod and
quotient.
        .word  MSTAR-4
        .byte  5,"*/MOD"
SSMOD
        $NEST
        .word  TOR,MSTAR,RFROM,MSMOD,EXIT

;    */ ( n1 n2 n3 -- q )
;       Multiply n1 by n2, then divide by n3. Return quotient
only.
        .word  SSMOD-6
        .byte  2,"*/",0
STASL
        $NEST
        .word  SSMOD,SWAP,DROP,EXIT
```

Miscellaneous Commands

1+	Increment tos by 1.
1-	Decrement tos by 1.
2+	Increment tos by 2.
2-	Decrement tos by 2.
2*	Multiply tos by 2.
2/	Divide tos by 2.
ALIGNED	Modify the byte address on top of the parameter stack so that it points to the next word boundary.
>CHAR	Convert a non-printable character to a harmless space character or a "~" (_ ASCII 126).
DEPTH	Push the number of items currently on the parameter stack to the top of the stack.
PICK	Take a number n off the parameter stack and replaces it with the n'th item on the parameter stack. The number n is 0-based; i.e., the top item is number 0, the next item is number 1, etc. Therefore, 0 PICK is equivalent to DUP, and 1 PICK is equivalent to OVER.

```
;; Miscellaneous

;    1+ ( a -- a+1 )
;       Increment.
;       .word  STASL-4
;       .byte  2,"1+",0
ONEP
        add    #1,tos
        $NEXT


;    1- ( a -- a-1 )
;       Decrement
;       .word  ONEP-4
;       .byte  2,"1-",0
ONEM
        sub    #1,tos
        $NEXT


;    2+ ( a -- a+2 )
;       Add cell size in byte to address.
;       .word  ONEM-4
;       .byte  2,"2+",0
CELLP
        add    #2,tos
        $NEXT


;    2- ( a -- a-2 )
;       Subtract cell size in byte from address.
;       .word  CELLP-4
;       .byte  2,"2-",0
CELLM
        sub    #2,tos
        $NEXT


;    2* ( n -- 2*n )
;       Multiply tos by cell size in bytes.
        .word  STASL-4
        .byte  2,"2*",0
```

```
CELLS
        rla     tos
        $NEXT


;   2/ ( n -- n/2 )
;       Divide tos by cell size in bytes.
        .word   CELLS-4
        .byte   2,"2/",0
TWOSL:
        rra     tos
        $NEXT


;   ALIGNED   ( b -- a )
;       Align address to the cell boundary.
;       .word   TWOSL-4
;       .byte   7,"ALIGNED"
ALGND
        add     #1,tos
        bic     #1,tos
        $NEXT


;   >CHAR     ( c -- c )
;       Filter non-printing characters.
;       .word   ALGND-8
;       .byte   5,">CHAR"
TCHAR
        $NEST
        .word   BLANK,MAX       ;mask msb
        .word   DOLIT,126,MIN ;check for printable
        .word   EXIT


;   DEPTH     ( -- n )
;       Return the depth of the data stack.
        .word   TWOSL-4
        .byte   5,"DEPTH"
DEPTH
        mov     stack,temp0
        pushs
        mov     #SPP,tos
```

```
        sub     temp0,tos
        rra     tos
        $NEXT


;   PICK        ( ... +n -- ... w )
;       Copy the nth stack item to tos.
        .word  DEPTH-6
        .byte  4,"PICK",0
PICK
        rla     tos
        add stack,tos
        mov     @tos,tos
        $NEXT
```

4.3 Text Interpreter

Here comes the heavy stuff.

A Forth command has two different representations: an internal representation in the form of a token, which specify the execution behavior of this command; and an external representation in the form of a name, which you can understand, and you can use it request a Forth Virtual Machine to do work. Both representations are store in memory in a record of this command.

This record has a name field storing the name of this command, and a code field storing executable code. All command records are linked through their link fields, so that commands can be searched in the memory. If a command is found in memory by its name, its token is the code field address, which provides its execution behavior. If a token, an execution address, is known, the corresponding name can also be found easily.

In most other programming languages, the primary goal of the language is to produce execution code. Procedures, constants and variables are giving names only for programming purposes. Once execution code is produced and verified, procedure names are not retained in the execution code, as they no more serve any useful purpose. Forth language is different, because its commands are built one upon another, and all commands may be called later to provide necessary services.

Command names are retained so that they can be referenced by name for interpretation and for compilation.

A text interpreter allows a user to interpret a command; ie., from the name of a command to find its token, and to execute or compile this token.

The Forth text interpreter is much more powerful than just finding and executing a single command from its name. In the interpretive mode, it interprets a list of Forth command names as a sequence of name strings. In the compiling mode, it converts a list of Forth command names into a list of tokens and builds a new Forth compound command to replace the list of commands.

You add new commands continually to your Forth system until the last command becomes your application.

In this section, I like to show you how to build this text interpreter which can interpret or execute a sequence of Forth commands in the form of a list of names:

    <name1>   <name2>   <name3>   ...   <nameN>

In the next section, I will show you how to enhance this text interpreter to compile new Forth commands in the following form:

    :   <new_command>   <name1>   <name2>   <name3>   ...   <nameN>   ;

Let me summarize what the text interpreter is doing:

Step 1. Accept one line of text from the terminal.
Step 2. Parse out a space delimited name string from input line.
Step 3. Search the memory for a command of this name.
Step 4. If it is a command, execute it. Go to Step 8.
Step 5. If it is not a command, convert it to a number.
Step 6. If it is a number, push it on parameter stack. Go to Step 8.
Step 7. If it is not a number, abort. Go back to step 1.
Step 8. If the text line is not exhausted, go back to step 2.
Step 9. If the text line is exhausted, go back to Step 1.

It looks very complicated. Yes, it is complicated, and we will discuss all the commands leading to the text interpreter. But, it is an operating system! Have you ever read the source code of an operating system? Very few people did. Very few people wrote operating systems. Here I will show you how to write this Forth operating system.

We will do query, parse, search, number conversions, terminal input, terminal output, command execution, and everything in between.

All these are important topics in computer sciences, requiring many years of intense studying. You will learn and master them, hopefully in a week.

Be patient, and follow the code.

Need to see a flow chart? You had seen it already. It was in the figure on COLD I showed you in Section 4.1 on the reset handler. It was not a flow chart you used to see, but it is a flow chart nonetheless. It not only shows the text interpreter. It also shows the command compiler as well.

Memory Access

A memory array is generally specified by its starting address and its length in bytes.

In a count string, the first byte is a count byte, specifying the number of bytes in the following string. String literals in compound commands and name strings in the headers of command records are all represented by count strings.

Following commands are useful in accessing memory arrays and strings.

+!	Add the second item on the parameter stack to the cell addressed by the top item on the stack.
COUNT	Fetch one byte from RAM memory pointed to by the address on the top of the parameter stack. This address is incremented by 1, and the byte just read is pushed on the stack. COUNT is designed to get the count byte at the beginning of a counted string, and returns the address of the first byte in the string and the length of this string. However, it is often used in a loop to read consecutive bytes in a byte array.
CMOVE	Copy a byte array from one location to another in memory. The top three items on the parameter stack are the source address, the destination address and the number of bytes to be copied.
FILL	Fill a memory array with the same byte. The top three items on the parameter stack are the address of the array, the length of the array in bytes, and the byte value to be filled into this array.

```
;; Memory access

;   +! ( n a -- )
;       Add n to the contents at address a.
        .word  PICK-6
        .byte  2,"+!",0
PSTOR
        add  @stack+,0(tos)
        pops
        $NEXT


;   COUNT      ( b -- b +n )
;       Return count byte of a string and add 1 to byte address.
        .word  PSTOR-4
        .byte  5,"COUNT"
COUNT
        mov.b  @tos+,temp0
        pushs
        mov    temp0,tos
        $NEXT


;   CMOVE      ( b1 b2 u -- )
;       Copy u bytes from b1 to b2.
        .word  COUNT-6
        .byte  5,"CMOVE"
CMOVE:
        mov    @stack+,temp0 ;destination
        mov    @stack+,temp1 ;source
        jmp    CMOVE2
CMOVE1:
        mov.b  @temp1+,0(temp0)
        inc    temp0
CMOVE2:
        dec    tos
        jn     CMOVE3 ;I need a jp.  Oh, well.
        jmp    CMOVE1
CMOVE3:
        JMP    DROP
```

```
;    FILL       ( b u c -- )
;       Fill u bytes of character c to area beginning at b.
        .word   CMOVE-6
        .byte   4,"FILL",0
FILL:
        mov     @stack+,temp0 ;count
        mov     @stack+,temp1 ;destination
        jmp     FIL2
FIL1:
        mov.b   tos,0(temp1)
        inc     temp1
FIL2:
        dec     temp0
        jn      FIL3
        jmp     FIL1
FIL3:
        JMP     DROP
```

User Variables

In 430eForth v4.3, all variables used by the system are merged together and are called user variables. They are stored in a RAM memory array starting at location $200. Their initial values are stored in flash information memory, Segment D, starting at location $1000.

In the original design of the eForth Mode, Bill Muench was very ambitious to lay down the structures of a multitasking system which could support many users and many tasks concurrently. Each user or task would have its own stacks and variables. These variables were therefore called user variables. 430eForth v4.3 is a single user system, but the terminology stuck.

When you finish coding your application, copy these variables back to Segment D, and your application, hopefully, will boot up on reset.

Variable	Address	Function
'BOOT	200H	Execution vector to start application command.
BASE	202H	Radix base for numeric conversion.

tmp	204H	Scratch pad.
HLD	206H	Pointer to a buffer holding next digit for numeric conversion.
>IN	208H	Input buffer character pointer used by text interpreter.
#TIB	20AH	Number of characters in input buffer.
'TIB	20CH	Address of Terminal Input Buffer.
'EVAL	20EH	Execution vector switching between $INTERPRET and $COMPILE.
CONTEXT	210H	Vocabulary array pointing to last name fields of dictionary.
CP	212H	Pointer to top of dictionary, the first available flash memory location to compile new command
DP	214H	Pointer to the first available RAM memory location.
LAST	216H	Pointer to name field of last command in dictionary.

```
;; User variables

;    'BOOT      ( -- a )
;        The application startup vector.
         .word  FILL-6
         .byte  5,"'BOOT"
TBOOT
         $CONST
         .word  200H


;    BASE       ( -- a )
;        Storage of the radix base for numeric I/O.
         .word  TBOOT-6
         .byte  4,"BASE",0
BASE
         $CONST
         .word  202H
```

```
;   tmp       ( -- a )
;       A temporary storage location used in parse and find.
;       .word  BASE-6
;       .byte  COMPO+3,"tmp"
TEMP
      $CONST
      .word  204H


;   #TIB      ( -- a )
;       Hold the character pointer while parsing input stream.
;       .word  BASE-6
;       .byte  4,"#TIB",0
NTIB
      $CONST
      .word  206H


;   >IN       ( -- a )
;       Hold the character pointer while parsing input stream.
;       .word  NTIB-6
;       .byte  3,">IN"
INN
      $CONST
      .word  208H


;   HLD       ( -- a )
;       Hold a pointer in building a numeric output string.
;       .word  INN-4
;       .byte  3,"HLD"
HLD
      $CONST
      .word  20AH


;   'EVAL     ( -- a )
;       A area to specify vocabulary search order.
;       .word  HLD-4
;       .byte  5,"'EVAL"
TEVAL
      $CONST
      .word  20CH
```

```
;    CONTEXT   ( -- a )
;       A area to specify vocabulary search order.
;       .word  TEVAL-6
;       .byte  7,"CONTEXT"
CNTXT
        $CONST
        .word  20EH


;    CP ( -- a )
;       Point to the top of the code dictionary.
        .word  BASE-6
        .byte  2,"CP",0
CP
        $CONST
        .word  210H


;    DP ( -- a )
;       Point to the bottom of the free ram area.
        .word  CP-4
        .byte  2,"DP",0
DP
        $CONST
        .word  212H


;    LAST      ( -- a )
;       Point to the last name in the name dictionary.
;       .word  DP-4
;       .byte  4,"LAST",0
LAST
        $CONST
        .word  214H
```

Numeric Output

Forth is interesting in its special capabilities in handling numbers across a man-machine interface. It recognizes that machines and humans prefer very different representations of numbers. Machines prefer binary representation, but humans prefer decimal Arabic representation. However, depending on circumstances, you may want numbers to be represented in other radices, like hexadecimal, octal, and sometimes binary.

Forth solves this problem of incompatible internal (machine) versus external (human) number representations by insisting that all numbers are represented in binary form in CPU and memory. Only when numbers are imported or exported for human consumption are they converted to external ASCII representation. The radix of the external representation is stored in a user variable BASE. You can select any reasonable radix in BASE, 2 up to 72, limited by available printable characters in the ASCII character set. My favorite radix is 19, number of horizontal and vertical lines on a GO game board.

The output number string is built below the PAD buffer in RAM memory. The least significant digit is extracted from the integer on the top of the parameter stack by dividing it by the current radix in BASE. The digit thus extracted is added to the output string backwards from PAD to the low memory. The conversion is terminated when the integer is divided to zero. The address and length of the number string are made available by #> for outputting.

An output number conversion is initiated by <# and terminated by #>. Between them, # converts one digit at a time, #S converts all the digits, while HOLD and SIGN inserts special characters into the string under construction. This set of commands is very versatile and can handle all imaginable output formats.

The following figure show how a number 12345 on top of parameter stack is converted to a number string 123.45 in the number buffer, ready to be typed out to a terminal:

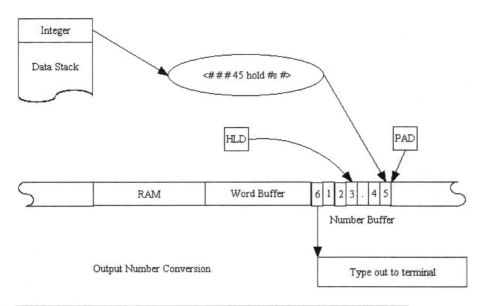

Output Number Conversion

HERE	Push the address of the first free location in the RAM memory. Forth text interpreter stores here a string parsed out of the Terminal Input Buffer and then searches the dictionary for a command with this name.
PAD	Push on the parameter stack the address of the text buffer where numbers to be output are constructed and text strings are stored temporarily. It is 64 bytes above HERE.
TIB	Push the address of the Terminal Input Buffer on the parameter stack. Terminal Input Buffer stores a line of text from the serial I/O input device. Forth text interpreter then processes or interprets this line of text.

```
;    HERE      ( -- a )
;        Return the top of the code dictionary.
         .word  DP-4
         .byte  4,"HERE",0
HERE
         $NEST
         .word  DP,AT,EXIT

;    PAD       ( -- a )
```

```
;        Return the address of a temporary buffer.
         .word  HERE-6
         .byte  3,"PAD"
PAD
         $NEST
         .word  HERE,DOLIT,80,PLUS,EXIT


;    TIB        ( -- a )
;        Return the address of the terminal input buffer.
         .word  PAD-4
         .byte  3,"TIB"
TIB
         $CONST
         .word  TIBB
```

DIGIT	Convert an integer digit to the corresponding ASCII character.
EXTRACT	Extract the least significant digit from a number n on the top of the parameter stack. n is divided by the radix in BASE and the extracted digit is converted to its ASCII character which is pushed on the parameter stack.
<#	Initiate the output number conversion process by storing PAD buffer address into user variable HLD, which points to the location next numeric digit will be stored.
HOLD	Append an ASCII character whose code is on the top of the parameter stack, to the numeric out put string at HLD. HLD is decremented to receive the next digit.
#	Extract one digit from integer on the top of the parameter stack, according to radix in BASE, and add it to output numeric string.
#S	Extract all digits to output string until the integer on the top of the parameter stack is divided down to 0.
SIGN	Insert a - sign into the numeric output string if the integer on the top of the parameter stack is negative.
#>	Terminate the numeric conversion and pushes the address and length of output numeric string on the parameter stack.
str	Convert a signed integer on the top of the parameter stack to a numeric output string.
HEX	Set numeric conversion radix to 16 for hexadecimal conversions.
DECIMAL	Set numeric conversion radix to 10 for decimal conversions.

```
;; Numeric output, single precision

;    DIGIT      ( u -- c )
;        Convert digit u to a character.
;        .word  LAST-6
;        .byte  5,"DIGIT"
DIGIT:
        cmp    #10,tos
        jl     DIGIT1
        add    #7,tos
DIGIT1:
        add    #"0",tos
        $NEXT


;    EXTRACT   ( n base -- n c )
;        Extract the least significant digit from n.
;        .word  DIGIT-6
;        .byte  7,"EXTRACT"
EXTRC
        $NEST
        .word  DOLIT,0,SWAP,UMMOD
        .word  SWAP,DIGIT,EXIT


;    <# ( -- )
;        Initiate the numeric output process.
;        .word  TIB-4
;        .byte  2,"<#",0
BDIGS
        $NEST
        .word  PAD,HLD,STORE,EXIT


;    HOLD       ( c -- )
;        Insert a character into the numeric output string.
;        .word  BDIGS-4
;        .byte  4,"HOLD",0
HOLD
        $NEST
        .word  HLD,AT,ONEM
        .word  DUPP,HLD,STORE,CSTOR,EXIT
```

```
;   #  ( u -- u )
;       Extract one digit from u and append the digit to output
string.
        .word  HOLD-6
        .byte  1,"#"
DIG
        $NEST
        .word  BASE,AT,EXTRC,HOLD,EXIT

;   #S ( u -- 0 )
;       Convert u until all digits are added to the output string.
        .word  DIG-2
        .byte  2,"#S",0
DIGS
        $NEST
DIGS1:
        .word  DIG,DUPP,QBRAN,DIGS2
        .word  BRAN,DIGS1
DIGS2:
        .word  EXIT

;   SIGN      ( n -- )
;       Add a minus sign to the numeric output string.
        .word  DIGS-4
        .byte  4,"SIGN",0
SIGN
        $NEST
        .word  ZLESS,QBRAN,SIGN1
        .word  DOLIT,"-",HOLD
SIGN1:
        .word  EXIT

;   #> ( w -- b u )
;       Prepare the output string to be TYPE'd.
        .word  SIGN-6
        .byte  2,"#",3EH,0
EDIGS
        $NEST
```

```
        .word   DROP,HLD,AT
        .word   PAD,OVER,SUBB,EXIT

;   str         ( n -- b u )
;       Convert a signed integer to a numeric string.
;       .word   EDIGS-4
;       .byte   3,"str"
STR
        $NEST
        .word   DUPP,TOR,ABSS
        .word   BDIGS,DIGS,RFROM
        .word   SIGN,EDIGS,EXIT

;   HEX         ( -- )
;       Use radix 16 as base for numeric conversions.
        .word   EDIGS-4
        .byte   3,"HEX"
HEX:
        mov     #16,&0x202
        $NEXT

;   DECIMAL     ( -- )
;       Use radix 10 as base for numeric conversions.
        .word   HEX-4
        .byte   7,"DECIMAL"
DECIM
        mov     #10,&0x202
        $NEXT
```

Numeric Input

The 430eForth text interpreter must handle numbers input to the system. It parses commands out of the input stream and executes them in sequence. When the text interpreter encounters a string which is not the name of a command in memory, it assumes that the string must be a number and attempts to convert the character string to a number according to the current radix. When the text interpreter succeeds in converting the string to a number, the number is pushed on the parameter stack for future use, if the text interpreter is in the interpreting mode. If it is in the compiling mode, the text interpreter will compile the number to memory as an integer literal so that when the command under construction is later executed, the integer value will be pushed on the parameter stack.

If the text interpreter fails to convert the string to a number, this is an error condition which will cause the text interpreter to abort, post an error message to you, discard the current input line of text, and then wait for your next line of commands.

The following figure show how a number string 123456 parsed out of the input buffer is converted to a number and pushed on the parameter stack:

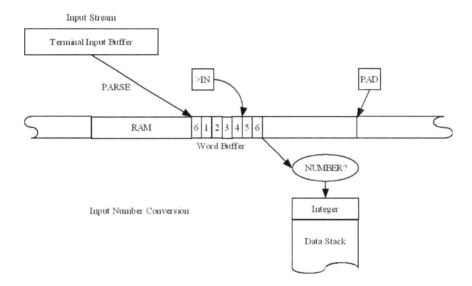

DIGIT?	Convert an ASCII numeric digit c on the top of the parameter stack to its numeric value u according to current radix b. If conversion is successful, push a true flag above u. If not successful, return c and a false flag.
NUMBER?	Convert a count string of ASCII numeric digits at location a to an integer. If first character is a $, convert in hexadecimal; otherwise, convert using radix in BASE. If first character is a -, negate converted integer. If an illegal character is encountered, the address of string and a false flag are pushed on the parameter stack. Successful conversion pushes integer value and a true

> flag on the parameter stack. NUMBER? is very complicated because it has to cover many formats in the input numeric string. It also has to detect the error condition when it encounters an illegal numeric digit. .

```
;; Numeric input, single precision

;    DIGIT?   ( c base -- u t )
;       Convert a character to its numeric value. A flag indicates
success.
;         .word  DECIM-8
;         .byte  6,"DIGIT?",0
DIGTQ
          mov    @stack,temp0
          sub    #"0",temp0
          jl     FALSE1
          cmp    #10,temp0
          jl     DIGTQ1
          sub    #7,temp0
DIGTQ1:
          cmp    tos,temp0
          mov    temp0,0(stack)
          jl     TRUE1
FALSE1:
          clr    tos
          $NEXT
TRUE1:
          mov    #-1,tos
          $NEXT


;    NUMBER?   ( a -- n T | a F )
;       Convert a number string to integer. Push a flag on tos.
          .word  DECIM-8
          .byte  7,"NUMBER?"
NUMBQ
          $NEST
          .word  BASE,AT,TOR,DOLIT,0,OVER,COUNT
          .word  OVER,CAT,DOLIT,'$',EQUAL,QBRAN,NUMQ1
```

```
        .word  HEX,SWAP,ONEP,SWAP,ONEM
NUMQ1:
        .word  OVER,CAT,DOLIT,'-',EQUAL,TOR
        .word  SWAP,RAT,SUBB,SWAP,RAT,PLUS,QDUP
        .word  QBRAN,NUMQ6
        .word  ONEM,TOR
NUMQ2:
        .word  DUPP,TOR,CAT,BASE,AT,DIGTQ
        .word  QBRAN,NUMQ4
        .word  SWAP,BASE,AT,STAR,PLUS,RFROM,ONEP
        .word  DONXT,NUMQ2
        .word  RAT,SWAP,DROP,QBRAN,NUMQ3
        .word  NEGAT
NUMQ3:
        .word  SWAP
        .word  BRAN,NUMQ5
NUMQ4:
        .word  RFROM,RFROM,DDROP,DDROP,DOLIT,0
NUMQ5:
        .word  DUPP
NUMQ6:
        .word  RFROM,DDROP,RFROM,BASE,STORE,EXIT
```

Terminal Output

430eForth v4.3 assumes that it communicates with you only through a serial I/O interface. To support the serial I/O, only three words are needed: ?KEY, KEY, and EMIT. These commands were discussed at the beginning of the kernel section. Terminal output commands are all derived from EMIT.

BL	Push a blank (space) character, ASCII 32 on parameter stack.
SPACE	Display a blank (space) character, ASCII 32.
CHARS	Display n ASCII characters. The ASCII code is on the top of the parameter stack, and number n is the second item on the parameter stack
SPACES	Display n blank (space) characters.

TYPE	Display n characters from a string in RAM memory. The second item on the parameter stack is the address of the string array, and the length in bytes is on the top of the parameter stack.
CR	Display a carriage-return and a line-feed, ASCII 13 and 10.

```
;; Terminal output

;    BL  ( -- 32 )
;        Return 32, the blank character.
         .word  NUMBQ-8
         .byte  2,"BL",0
BLANK
         $CONST
         .word  20H

;    SPACE     ( -- )
;        Send the blank character to the output device.
         .word  BLANK-4
         .byte  5,"SPACE"
SPACE
         $NEST
         .word  BLANK,EMIT,EXIT

;    SPACES    ( +n -- )
;        Send n spaces to the output device.
         .word  SPACE-6
         .byte  6,"SPACES",0
SPACS
         $NEST
         .word  DOLIT,0,MAX,TOR,BRAN,CHAR2
CHAR1:
         .word  SPACE
CHAR2:
         .word  DONXT,CHAR1,EXIT

;    TYPE      ( b u -- )
;        Output u characters from b.
         .word  SPACS-8
```

```
        .byte  4,"TYPE",0
TYPEE
        $NEST
        .word  TOR,BRAN,TYPE2
TYPE1:
        .word  DUPP,CAT,TCHAR,EMIT
        .word  ONEP
TYPE2:
        .word  DONXT,TYPE1
        .word  DROP,EXIT


;   CR ( -- )
;       Output a carriage return and a line feed.
        .word  TYPEE-6
        .byte  2,"CR",0
CR
        $NEST
        .word  DOLIT,CRR,EMIT
        .word  DOLIT,LF,EMIT,EXIT
```

String Output

We talked about integer literals and address literals. Here is one more: string literals. String literals are used to send out messages to alert the user, or to make text strings available for further processing at run time.

String literals are data structures compiled in compound command, in-line with other tokens, integer literals, address literals, and control structures. A string literal must start with a string token which knows how to handle the following string at run time. Here are two examples of string literals:

```
: xxx     ...    $" A compiled string"  ...   ;
: yyy     ...    ." An output string"  ...   ;
```

In compound command xxx, $" is an immediate command which compiles the following string as a string literal preceded by a special token $"|. When $"| is executed at run time, it returns the address of this string on the parameter stack. In yyy, ." compiles a string literal preceded by another token ."|, which displays the compiled string to the terminal at run time.

do$	Push the address of a string literal on the parameter stack. It is called by a string token like $"| or ."|, which precede their respective strings in flash memory. Therefore, the second item on the return stack points to the string. This address is pushed on the parameter stack. This second item on the return stack must be modified so that it will point to the next token after the string literal. This way. the token after the string literal will be executed, skipping over the string literal. Both $"\| and ."\| use the command do$, which retrieve the address of a string stored as the second item on the return stack.
$"|	Push the address of the following string on the parameter stack, and then executes the token immediately following the string.
."|	Display the following string, and then executes the token immediately following the string.

```
;    do$        ( -- a )
;        Return the address of a compiled string.
;        .word   CR-4
;        .byte   COMPO+3,"do$"
DOSTR
         $NEST
         .word   RFROM,RAT,RFROM,COUNT,PLUS
         .word   ALGND,TOR,SWAP,TOR,EXIT

;    $"|        ( -- a )
;        Run time routine compiled by $". Return address of a
compiled string.
;        .word   CR-4
;        .byte   COMPO+3,"$"""|"
STRQP
         $NEST
         .word   DOSTR,EXIT     ;force a call to do$

;    ."|        ( -- )
;        Run time routine of ." . Output a compiled string.
;        .word   STRQP-4
;        .byte   COMPO+3,".""" |"
DOTQP
         $NEST
         .word   DOSTR,COUNT,TYPEE,EXIT
```

Display Output Numbers

With the number formatting command set as shown above, one can format numbers for output in any format you can imagine. The free output format is a number string preceded by a single space. The fix column format displays a number right-justified in a column of a pre-determined width. The commands . , U., and ? use the free format. The commands .R and U.R use the fix column format.

.R	Display a signed integer n , the second item on the parameter stack, right-justified in a field of +n characters. +n is on the top of the parameter stack.
U.R	Display an unsigned integer n right-justified in a field of +n characters.
U.	Display an unsigned integer u in free format, followed by a space.
.	Display a signed integer n in free format, followed by a space.
?	Display signed integer stored in memory a on the top of the parameter stack, in free format followed by a space.

```
;     .R ( n +n -- )
;         Display an integer in a field of n columns, right
justified.
          .word  CR-4
          .byte  2,".R",0
DOTR
          $NEST
          .word  TOR,STR,RFROM,OVER,SUBB
          .word  SPACS,TYPEE,EXIT

;    U.R        ( u +n -- )
;         Display an unsigned integer in n column, right justified.
          .word  DOTR-4
          .byte  3,"U.R"
UDOTR
          $NEST
          .word  TOR,BDIGS,DIGS,EDIGS
          .word  RFROM,OVER,SUBB,SPACS,TYPEE,EXIT
```

```
;    U. ( u -- )
;        Display an unsigned integer in free format.
         .word  UDOTR-4
         .byte  2,"U.",0
UDOT
         $NEST
         .word  BDIGS,DIGS,EDIGS,SPACE,TYPEE,EXIT


;    .  ( w -- )
;        Display an integer in free format, preceeded by a space.
         .word  UDOT-4
         .byte  1,"."
DOT
         $NEST
         .word  BASE,AT,DOLIT,10,XORR        ;?decimal
         .word  QBRAN,DOT1
         .word  UDOT,EXIT        ;no, display unsigned
DOT1:    .word  STR,SPACE,TYPEE,EXIT             ;yes, display signed


;    ? ( a -- )
;        Display the contents in a memory cell.
         .word  DOT-2
         .byte  1,"?"
QUEST
         $NEST
         .word  AT,DOT,EXIT
```

Parsing

Parsing is always considered a very advanced topic in computer science. However, because Forth uses very simple syntax rules, parsing is easy. Forth input stream consists of ASCII strings separated by spaces and other white space characters like tabs, carriage returns, and line feeds. The text interpreter scans the input stream, parses out strings, and interprets them in sequence. After a string is parsed out of the input stream, the text interpreter will 'interpret' it; i.e., execute it if it is a valid command, compile it if the text interpreter is in the compiling mode, and convert it to a number if the string is not a Forth command.

The case where the delimiting character is a space (ASCII 32) is special, because this is when the text interpreter is parsing out a name for a new command. It thus must skip over leading space characters. When parse is used to compile string literals, it will use a double quote character (ASCII 34) as the delimiting character. If the delimiting character is not a space, the parser starts scanning immediately, looking for the designated delimiting character.

An example of parsing out an integer 16 in a text string is shown as follows:

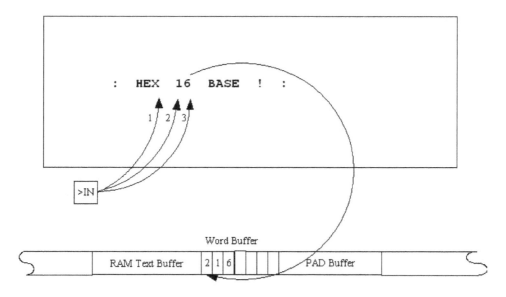

1. Start scanning after HEX in the Input Buffer.
2. Skip leading blank characters.
3. Scan string to next blank character.
4. Copy the parsed string into the Word Buffer.

parse	The elementary command to do text parsing. From the input stream, which starts at b1 and is of u1 characters long, it parses out the first text string delimited by character c. It returns the address b2 and length u2 of the string just parsed out and the difference n between b1 and b2.
PARSE	Scan the input stream in the Terminal Input Buffer from where >IN points to, until the end of the buffer, for a string

	delimited by character c. It returns the address and length of the string parsed out. PARSE calls parse to do the detailed works. PARSE is used to implement many specialized parsing commands to perform different parsing functions.
.(	Display the following string till the next) character. It is used to display text on the terminal.
(	Discard the following string till the next) character. It is used to place comments in source code.
\	Discard all characters till end of a line. It is used to insert comment lines in source code.
CHAR	Parse the next string out but returns only the first character in this string. It gets an ASCII character from the input stream.
TOKEN	Parse out the next string delimited by space character. It then copies this string as a counted string to the first free area in RAM memory and returns its address. The length of the string is limited to 31 characters.
WORD	Parse out the next string delimited by the ASCII character c. It then copies this string as a counted string to the first free area in RAM memory and returns its address. The length of the string is limited to 255 characters.

```
;; Parsing

;    parse      ( b u c -- b u delta ; <string> )
;        Scan string delimited by c. Return found string and its
offset.
;          .word  QUEST-2
;          .byte  5,"parse"
PARS
          $NEST
          .word  TEMP,STORE,OVER,TOR,DUPP,QBRAN,PARS8
          .word  ONEM,TEMP,AT,BLANK,EQUAL,QBRAN,PARS3
          .word  TOR
PARS1:
          .word  BLANK,OVER,CAT          ;skip leading blanks ONLY
          .word  SUBB,ZLESS,INVER,QBRAN,PARS2
          .word  ONEP,DONXT,PARS1
```

```
        .word  RFROM,DROP,DOLIT,0,DUPP,EXIT
PARS2:
        .word  RFROM
PARS3:
        .word  OVER,SWAP,TOR
PARS4:
        .word  TEMP,AT,OVER,CAT,SUBB       ;scan for delimiter
        .word  TEMP,AT,BLANK,EQUAL,QBRAN,PARS5
        .word  ZLESS
PARS5:
        .word  QBRAN,PARS6
        .word  ONEP,DONXT,PARS4
        .word  DUPP,TOR,BRAN,PARS7
PARS6:
        .word  RFROM,DROP,DUPP,ONEP,TOR
PARS7:
        .word  OVER,SUBB,RFROM,RFROM,SUBB,EXIT
PARS8:
        .word  OVER,RFROM,SUBB,EXIT


;   PARSE    ( c -- b u ; <string> )
;       Scan input stream and return counted string delimited by
c.
;       .word  QUEST-2
;       .byte  5,"PARSE"
PARSE
        $NEST
        .word  TOR,TIB,INN,AT,PLUS ;current input buffer pointer
        .word  NTIB,AT,INN,AT,SUBB ;remaining count
        .word  RFROM,PARS,INN,PSTOR,EXIT


;   .( ( -- )
;       Output following string up to next ) .
        .word  QUEST-2
        .byte  IMEDD+2,".(",0
DOTPR
        $NEST
        .word  DOLIT,")",PARSE,TYPEE,EXIT
```

```
;    (   ( -- )
;        Ignore following string up to next ) . A comment.
         .word  DOTPR-4
         .byte  IMEDD+1,"("
PAREN
         $NEST
         .word  DOLIT,")",PARSE,DDROP,EXIT


;    \  ( -- )
;        Ignore following text till the end of line.
         .word  PAREN-2
         .byte  IMEDD+1,"\"
BKSLA
         $NEST
         .word  NTIB,AT,INN,STORE,EXIT


;    CHAR     ( -- c )
;        Parse next word and return its first character.
         .word  BKSLA-2
         .byte  4,"CHAR",0
CHAR
         $NEST
         .word  BLANK,PARSE,DROP,CAT,EXIT


;    TOKEN    ( -- a ; <string> )
;        Parse  a  word  from  input  stream  and  copy  it  to  name
dictionary.
         .word  CHAR-6
         .byte  5,"TOKEN"
TOKEN
         $NEST
         .word  BLANK,PARSE,DOLIT,31,MIN
TOKEN1
         .word  HERE,DDUP,CSTOR,ONEP
         .word  SWAP,CMOVE,HERE
         .word  DOLIT,0,HERE,COUNT,PLUS,CSTOR,EXIT
```

```
;    WORD      ( c -- a ; <string> )
;       Parse  a  word  from  input  stream  and  copy  it  to  code
dictionary.
        .word  TOKEN-6
        .byte  4,"WORD",0
WORDD
        $NEST
        .word  PARSE,BRAN,TOKEN1
```

Dictionary Search

In 430eForth v4.3, command records in flash memory are linearly linked into a dictionary. A command record contains three fields: a link field holding the name field address of the previous command record, a name field holding the name as a counted string, and a code field holding executable code and data. A dictionary search follows the linked list of records to find a name which matches a text string. It returns the name field address and the code field address, if a match is found.

The link field of the first command record contains a 0, indicating it is the end of the linked list. A user variable CONTEXT holds an address pointing to the name field of the last command record. The dictionary search starts at CONTEXT and terminates at the first matched name, or at the first command record.

From CONTEXT, we locate the name field of the last command record in the dictionary. It this name does not match the string to be searched, we can find the link field of this record, which is 2 bytes less than the name field address. From the link field, we locate the name field of the next command record. Compare the name with the search string. And so forth. We will either find a command or reach the end of the linked list.

The linking of records in dictionary is show in the following figure:

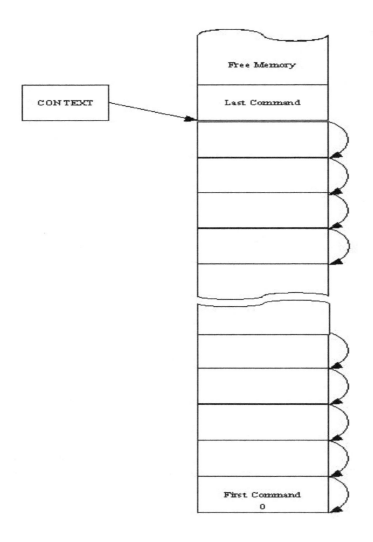

NAME>	Convert a name field address in a command record to the code field address of this command record. Code field address is the name field address plus length of name plus one, and aligned to the next cell boundary.
SAME?	Compare two strings at addresses a and b for u bytes. It returns a 0 if two strings are equal. It returns a positive

	integer if a string is greater than b string. It returns a negative integer if a string is less than b string.
NAME?	Search the dictionary starting at CONTEXT for a name string at address a. Return the code field address ca and name field address na if a matched command is found. Otherwise, return the original string address a and a false flag. Assume that a count string is at memory address a, and the name field address of the last command record is in address va. If the string matches the name of a command, both the code field address and the name field address of the command record are returned. If the string is not a valid command, the original string address and a false flag are returned. It runs the dictionary search very quickly, because it first compares the length byte and the first character in the name field as a 16 bit integer. In most cases of mismatch, this comparison would fail and the next record can be reached through the link field. If the first two characters match, then SAME? is invoked to compare the rest of the name field, one byte at a time.

```
;; Dictionary search

;    NAME>    ( na -- ca )
;        Return a code address given a name address.
;        .word  WORDD-6
;        .byte  5,"NAME>"
NAMET
         mov.b  @tos+,temp0
         and    #0x1F,temp0
         add    temp0,tos
         inc    tos
         bic    #1,tos
         $NEXT

;    SAME?    ( a a -- a a f \ -0+ )
;        Compare u cells in two strings. Return 0 if identical.
;        .word  NAMET-6
;        .byte  5,"SAME?"
SAMEQ
```

```
        pushs
        mov     2(stack),tos
        mov.b   @tos,tos
SAME1:
        mov     2(stack),temp0
        add     tos,temp0
        mov.b   0(temp0),temp0
        mov     0(stack),temp1
        add     tos,temp1
        mov.b   0(temp1),temp1
        sub     temp1,temp0
        jnz     SAME2
        dec     tos
        jnz     SAME1
        $NEXT
SAME2:
        jmp TRUE1

;   NAME?    ( a -- ca na | a F )
;       Search all context vocabularies for a string.
;       .word  WORDD-6
;       .byte  5,"NAME?"
NAMEQ
        $NEST
        .word  CNTXT,AT
FIND1:
        .word  DUPP,QBRAN,FIND3     ;end of dictionary
        .word  OVER,AT,OVER,AT,DOLIT,MASKK,ANDD,EQUAL
        .word  QBRAN,FIND4
        .word  SAMEQ,QBRAN,FIND2    ;match
FIND4:
        .word  CELLM,AT,BRAN,FIND1
FIND2:
        .word  SWAP,DROP,DUPP,NAMET,SWAP,EXIT
FIND3:
        .word  EXIT
```

Terminal Input

The text interpreter interprets source text you type on a terminal and stored all the characters received in a Terminal Input Buffer. We all make mistakes typing on a terminal. The text interpreter must allow some simple editing effort on your part, like backspaces to erase a few characters just typed.

To edit characters in the Terminal Input Buffer, we need special commands to deal with backspace character and carriage return: On top of stack, three special parameters are referenced in many commands: bot is the Beginning Of the Text input buffer, eot is the End Of the Text input buffer, and cur points to the current character in the input buffer.

QUERY is the final command accepting a line of text into the Terminal Input Buffer, terminating by a carriage return or enter.

^H	Process back-space character (ASCII 8). It erases the last character entered, and decrement the character pointer cur. If cur=bot, do nothing because you cannot backup beyond beginning of input buffer.
TAP	Display character c to terminal, store c in cur, and increment the character pointer cur, which points to the current character in the input buffer. bot and eot are pointing to the beginning and end of the input buffer.
kTAP	Process character c. bot is pointing at the beginning of the input buffer, and eot is pointing at the end. cur points to the current character in the input buffer. The character c is normally stored at cur, which is then incremented by 1. If c is a carriage-return (ASCII 13), echo a space and make eot=cur., thus terminating the input process If c is a back-space (ASCII 8), erase the last character and decrement cur.
ACCEPT	Accept u characters into an input buffer starting at address b, or until a carriage return (ASCII 13) is encountered. The value of u returned is the actual number of characters received.
QUERY	Accept up to 80 characters from the input device to the Terminal Input Buffer. It also prepares the Terminal Input Buffer for parsing by setting #TIB to the length of the input text stream, and clearing >IN which points to the beginning of the Terminal Input Buffer.

```
;; Terminal input

;    ^H ( bot eot cur -- bot eot cur )
;       Backup the cursor by one character.
;       .word  NAMEQ-6
;       .byte  2,"^H",0
BKSP
        $NEST
        .word  TOR,OVER,RFROM,SWAP,OVER,XORR
        .word  QBRAN,BACK1
        .word  DOLIT,BKSPP,EMIT,ONEM
        .word  BLANK,EMIT,DOLIT,BKSPP,EMIT
BACK1:
        .word  EXIT

;    TAP      ( bot eot cur c -- bot eot cur )
;       Accept and echo the key stroke and bump the cursor.
;       .word  BKSP-4
;       .byte  3,"TAP"
TAP
        $NEST
        .word  DUPP,EMIT,OVER,CSTOR,ONEP,EXIT

;    kTAP     ( bot eot cur c -- bot eot cur )
;       Process a key stroke, CR or backspace.
;       .word  TAP-4
;       .byte  4,"kTAP",0
KTAP
        $NEST
        .word  DUPP,DOLIT,CRR,XORR,QBRAN,KTAP2
        .word  DOLIT,BKSPP,XORR,QBRAN,KTAP1
        .word  BLANK,TAP,EXIT
KTAP1:
        .word  BKSP,EXIT
KTAP2:
        .word  DROP,SWAP,DROP,DUPP,EXIT

;    accept   ( b u -- b u )
```

```
;       Accept characters to input buffer. Return with actual
count.
        .word  WORDD-6
        .byte  6,"ACCEPT",0
ACCEP
        $NEST
        .word  OVER,PLUS,OVER
ACCP1:
        .word  DDUP,XORR,QBRAN,ACCP4
        .word  KEY,DUPP,BLANK,SUBB,DOLIT,95,ULESS
        .word  QBRAN,ACCP2
        .word  TAP,BRAN,ACCP1
ACCP2:
        .word  KTAP
ACCP3:
        .word  BRAN,ACCP1
ACCP4:
        .word  DROP,OVER,SUBB,EXIT


;    QUERY    ( -- )
;       Accept input stream to terminal input buffer.
        .word  ACCEP-8
        .byte  5,"QUERY"
QUERY
        $NEST
        .word  TIB,DOLIT,80,ACCEP,NTIB,STORE
        .word  DROP,DOLIT,0,INN,STORE,EXIT
```

Error Handling

In the original eForth Model, there was a very sophisticated THROW-CATCH mechanism to handle different types of errors and different ways to respond to them. It is not necessary for most microcontroller applications. In 430eForth v4.3, we have only one way to recover from error conditions, that is to return to the QUIT loop, the text interpreter in its interpretive mode.

When an error occurred, it is usually because the text interpreter encounters a string which cannot be interpreted or processed. This string usually is last parsed out and stored in a word buffer in RAM memory. The command ERROR is invoked to handle this error condition. ERROR displays this string followed by a ? mark as an error message. Then the text interpreter starts over. Stacks are cleared and then jump to QUIT.

ERROR	Display the string in RAM memory located at address a, followed by a ? mark and aborts. Abort means clearing the parameter stack, and returns to the text interpreter loop QUIT.
abort"	It is compiled as a sting literal with an error message in a compound command. When abort" is executed, it examines the top item on the parameter stack. It the flag is true, it displays the following error message and QUIT; otherwise, skip over the error message and continue execution the next token.

```
;; Error handling

; QUIT inits return stack. ERROR inits both stacks.

;    ERROR      ( a -- )
;        Return address of a null string with zero count.
;        .word  QUERY-6
;        .byte  5,"ERROR"
ERROR:
        $NEST
        .word  SPACE,COUNT,TYPEE,DOLIT
        .word  3FH,EMIT,CR,SPSTO,QUIT

;    abort"    ( f -- )
;        Run time routine of ABORT" . Abort with a message.
;        .word  ERROR-6
;        .byte  COMPO+6,"abort""",0
ABORQ
        $NEST
        .word  QBRAN,ABOR1    ;text flag
        .word  DOSTR,COUNT,TYPEE,SPSTO,QUIT        ;pass        error
string
ABOR1:
        .word  DOSTR,DROP,EXIT
```

Text Interpreter Loop

Text interpreter in Forth is like a conventional operating system of a computer. It is the primary interface you get the computer to do useful work. Since Forth uses very simple syntax rule--commands are separated by spaces, the text interpreter is also very simple. It accepts a line of text from the terminal, parses out a command delimited by spaces, locates the command in the dictionary and then executes it. The process is repeated until the input text is exhausted. Then the text interpreter waits for another line of text and interprets it again. This cycle repeats until you are exhausted and turn off the computer.

In 430eForth v4.3, the text interpreter is coded as the command QUIT. QUIT contains an infinite loop which repeats the QUERY-EVAL command pair. QUERY accepts a line of text from the input terminal. EVAL interprets the text one command at a time till the end of the text line.

$INTERPRET	Execute a command whose name string is stored at address a on the parameter stack. If the string is not a valid command, convert it to a number. Failing the numeric conversion, execute ERROR and return to QUIT.
[	Activate the text interpreter by storing the code field address of $INTERPRET into the variable 'EVAL, which is executed in EVAL while the text interpreter is in the interpretive mode.
.OK	Display the familiar ok prompting message after executing to the end of a line. The message ok is displayed only when the text interpreter is in the interpretive mode. While compiling, the prompt is suppressed.
?STACK	Check for stack underflow. Abort, resetting the parameter stack pointer, if the stack depth is negative.
EVAL	Parse commands from the input stream and invokes whatever token in 'EVAL to process the commands, either execute it with $INTERPRET or compile it with $COMPILE.
QUIT	This is the operating system, the text interpreter, or a shell, of the 430eForth system. It is an infinite loop Forth would never get out, normally. It uses QUERY to accept a line of commands from the input terminal and

then lets EVAL to parse out the commands and execute them. After a line is processed, it displays an ok message and waits for the next line of commands. When an error occurred during execution, it displays the string which caused the error as an error message. After the error is reported, it re-initializes the system by clearing the return stack and comes back to receive the next line of commands. Because the behavior of EVAL can be changed by storing either $INTERPRET or $COMPILE into 'EVAL, QUIT exhibits the dual nature of a text interpreter and a command compiler.

```
;; Text interpreter

;    $INTERPRET      ( a -- )
;        Interpret a word. If failed, try to convert it to an
integer.
;        .word   ERROR-6
;        .byte   10,"$INTERPRET",0
INTER
        $NEST
        .word   NAMEQ,QDUP      ;?defined
        .word   QBRAN,INTE1
        .word   AT,DOLIT,COMPO,ANDD  ;?compile only lexicon bits
        .word   ABORQ
        .byte   13," compile only"
        .word   EXECU,EXIT      ;execute defined word
INTE1:
        .word   NUMBQ  ;convert a number
        .word   QBRAN,INTE2,EXIT
INTE2:
        .word   ERROR  ;error


;    [  ( -- )
;        Start the text interpreter.
        .word   QUERY-6
        .byte   IMEDD+1,"["
LBRAC
        $NEST
```

```
        .word  DOLIT,INTER,TEVAL,STORE,EXIT

;    .OK       ( -- )
;       Display 'ok' only while interpreting.
;       .word  LBRAC-2
;       .byte  3,".OK"
DOTOK
        $NEST
        .word  DOLIT,INTER,TEVAL,AT,EQUAL
        .word  QBRAN,DOTO1
        .word  DOTQP
        .byte  3," ok"
DOTO1:  .word  CR,EXIT

;    ?STACK    ( -- )
;       Abort if the data stack underflows.
;       .word  DOTOK-4
;       .byte  6,"?STACK",0
QSTAC
        $NEST
        .word  DEPTH,ZLESS   ;check only for underflow
        .word  ABORQ
        .byte  10," underflow",0
        .word  EXIT

;    EVAL      ( -- )
;       Interpret the input stream.
;       .word  QSTAC-8
;       .byte  4,"EVAL",0
EVAL
        $NEST
EVAL1:
        .word  TOKEN,DUPP,CAT      ;?input stream empty
        .word  QBRAN,EVAL2
        .word  TEVAL,ATEXE,QSTAC   ;evaluate input, check stack
        .word  BRAN,EVAL1
EVAL2:
        .word  DROP,DOTOK,EXIT     ;prompt
```

```
;   QUIT        ( -- )
;       Reset return stack pointer and start text interpreter.
        .word  LBRAC-2
        .byte  4,"QUIT",0
QUIT
        $NEST
        .word  RPSTO,LBRAC   ;start interpretation
QUIT1:
        .word  QUERY,EVAL    ;get input
        .word  BRAN,QUIT1    ;continue till error
```

4.4 Command Compiler

In 430eForth v4.3, the command compiler is the twin brother of the text interpreter. They share lot of code and they reside in the same interpreter loop QUIT. Let us use the same task sequence in the text interpreter section to show what the command compiler does:

Step 1. Accept one line of text from the terminal.
Step 2. Parse out a space delimited name string from the input line.
Step 3. Search the dictionary for a command of this name.
Step 4. If it is an immediate command, execute it. Go to Step 9.
Step 5. If it is a command, compile it as a token. Go to Step 9.
Step 6. If it is not a command, convert it to a number.
Step 7. If it is a number, compile an integer literal. Go to Step 9.
Step 8. If it is not a number, abort. Go back to step 1.
Step 9. If the text line is not exhausted, go back to step 2.
Step 10. If the text line is exhausted, go back to Step 1.

Compiler and interpreter are both processing a linear list of names. However, interpreting is for talking, a single line of text is generally sufficient. Compiling is for writing, and it can express deeply convoluted thoughts and ideas, in many lines, or in many pages. These ideas cannot be expressed in a single line of text. You need a big sheet of paper, or a file, to put them down properly. In addition to compile linear lists of tokens, the command compile can build complicated branch structures, loop structures, and control structures embedded a token list. These structures are built with the immediate commands, which are executed immediately by the compiler. These are things we will discuss in this section.

Forth language assumes a van Neumann computer architecture, in which all memory locations are readable and writable, and that all memory location can store code and data. In this case, compiling new commands in memory is no problem. However, in MSP430G2553, there are only 512 bytes of RAM you can write freely.

The 16 KB of flash memory, where old commands are stored and new commands are to be added, is more difficult to write. The flash memory can only be erased in 512 byte pages. After erasing, bits in memory can only be cleared to 0. Cleared bits cannot be set individually. It makes compiling difficult, but we can work things out within these restrictions. After all, you pay what you get. In MSP430G2 LaunchPad, you did not pay much. You have to live within the limitations.

Flash Memory

In MSP430G2553, the flash main memory is organized in 512 byte pages, and the flash information memory is organized in 64 byte pages. The flash memory can be read like RAM memory, but to write and to erase flash memory, you have to go through the flash memory controller. The flash memory controller makes things easy. You first unlock the memory controller, and then issue a write or erase command. Then you write to one location in the selected flash memory page, and finally lock the flash memory controller. Following are the commands to write one 16-bit integer to a flash memory location, to erase one page of flash memory, and to copy an array from a memory area to a flash memory area.

ALLOT	Allocate n bytes of RAM memory on bottom of the free RAM space. User variable DP points to the bottom of free RAM space.
IALLOT	Allocate n bytes of flash memory on the top of the dictionary. User variable CP points to the top of the dictionary.
I!	Store a 16-bit data w in flash memory address a.
ERASE	Erase one 512 byte page of flash main memory or 64 bytes of flash information memory. The page address a is on the top of the parameter stack.
WRITE	Copy n bytes of one memory array, starting at address src, to an array in flash memory, starting at flash address dest. All addresses are byte addresses.

The command I! is actually the primitive flash memory programmer in 430eForth v4.3. It allows us to write into the flash memory to build new Forth commands. It is used to define the , (comma) command, which adds one more 16-bit integer to the top of the Forth dictionary, and thus extends the Forth system by one integer. Repeatedly adding data and instructions to the dictionary to form new Forth commands is what this command compiler does.

```
;; Compiler utilities

;   ALLOT      ( n -- )
;       Allocate n bytes to the RAM dictionary.
        .word   QUIT-6
        .byte   5,"ALLOT"
ALLOT
        $NEST
        .word   DP,PSTOR,EXIT ;adjust code pointer

;   IALLOT     ( n -- )
;       Allocate n bytes to the code dictionary.
        .word   ALLOT-6
        .byte   6,"IALLOT",0
IALLOT
        $NEST
        .word   CP,PSTOR,EXIT ;adjust code pointer

;   I! ( n a -- )
;       Store n to address a in code dictionary.
        .word   IALLOT-8
        .byte   2,"I!",0
ISTORE
        mov     #FWKEY,&FCTL3 ; Clear LOCK
        mov     #FWKEY+WRT,&FCTL1 ; Enable write
;       call    #STORE
        mov.w   @stack+,0(tos)
        pops
        mov     #FWKEY,&FCTL1 ; Done. Clear WRT
        mov     #FWKEY+LOCK,&FCTL3 ; Set LOCK
        $NEXT
```

```
;    ERASE    ( a -- )
;        Erase a segment at address a.
         .word  ISTORE-4
         .byte  5,"ERASE"
IERASE
         mov    #FWKEY,&FCTL3 ; Clear LOCK
         mov    #FWKEY+ERASE,&FCTL1 ; Enable erase
         clr    0(tos)
         mov    #FWKEY+LOCK,&FCTL3 ; Set LOCK
         pops
         $NEXT

;    WRITE    ( src dest n -- )
;        Copy n byte from src to dest.  Dest is in flash memory.
         .word  IERASE-6
         .byte  5,"WRITE"
WRITE
         $NEST
         .word  TWOSL,TOR
WRITE1
         .word  OVER,AT,OVER,ISTORE
         .word  CELLP,SWAP,CELLP,SWAP
         .word  DONXT,WRITE1
         .word  DDROP,EXIT
```

Compiler Commands

,	It is the most fundamental compiler command. It compiles an integer w to dictionary in the flash memory, and adds this integer to the growing token list of the current command under construction. This is the primitive compiler upon which the entire command compiler rests.
call,	Compile or assemble a subroutine call instruction with the execution address on the parameter stack as destination.

COMPILE	Compile the execution address of the next command in the token list. It forces compilation of the next token at run time.
LITERAL	Compile an integer literal. It first compiles a DOLIT token, followed by an integer value from the parameter stack. When DOLIT is executed, it extracts the integer in the token list and pushes it on the parameter stack.
$,"	Compile a string literal. String text is taken from the input stream and terminated by a double quote. A token $"| is compiled before the string to form a sting literal.

```
;    ,   ( w -- )
;       Compile an integer into the code dictionary.
        .word   WRITE-6
        .byte   1,","
COMMA
        $NEST
        .word   CP,AT,DUPP,CELLP      ;cell boundary
        .word   CP,STORE,ISTORE,EXIT

;    call,     ( w -- )
;       Compile a call instruction into the code dictionary.
;       .word   COMMA-2
;       .byte   5,"call,"
CALLC
        $NEST
        .word   DOLIT,CALLL,COMMA
        .word   COMMA,EXIT

;    [COMPILE] ( -- ; <string> )
;       Compile the next immediate word into code dictionary.
;       .word   COMMA-2
;       .byte   IMEDD+9,"[COMPILE]"
BCOMP
        $NEST
        .word   TICK,COMMA,EXIT

;    COMPILE   ( -- )
;       Compile the next address in colon list to code dictionary.
```

```
;       .word  BCOMP-10
;       .byte  COMPO+7,"COMPILE"
COMPI
        $NEST
        .word  RFROM,DUPP,AT,COMMA  ;compile address
        .word  CELLP,TOR,EXIT       ;adjust return address

;   LITERAL   ( w -- )
;       Compile tos to code dictionary as an integer literal.
;       .word  COMPI-8
;       .byte  IMEDD+7,"LITERAL"
LITER
        $NEST
        .word  COMPI,DOLIT,COMMA,EXIT

;   $,"       ( -- )
;       Compile a literal string up to next " .
;       .word  LITER-8
;       .byte  3,"$,"""
STRCQ
        $NEST
        .word  DOLIT,""""
        .word  WORDD  ;move string to code dictionary
        .word  STRCQ1,EXIT


STRCQ1
        $NEST
        .word  DUPP,CAT,TWOSL       ;calculate   aligned   end   of
string
        .word  TOR
STRCQ2
        .word  DUPP,AT,COMMA,CELLP
        .word  DONXT,STRCQ2
        .word  DROP,EXIT
```

Structure Commands

Immediate commands are not compiled as tokens by the compiler. Instead, they are executed by the compiler immediately. They are used to build literal and control structures in compound commands. Immediate commands has its IMMEDIATE lexicon bit set, in the length byte of the name field. The control structures used in 430eForth v4.3 are the following:

Conditional branch	IF ... THEN
	IF ... ELSE ... THEN
Finite loop	FOR ... NEXT
	FOR ... AFT ... THEN... NEXT
Infinite loop	BEGIN ... AGAIN
Indefinite loop	BEGIN ... UNTIL
	BEGIN ... WHILE ... REPEAT

They are also shown schematically in the following figure:

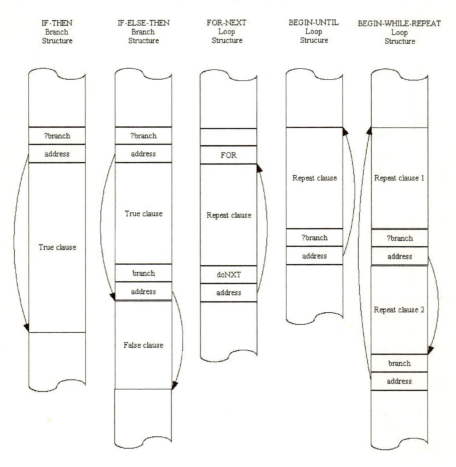

A control structure contains one or more address literals with BRAN, QBRAN and DONXT commands, which causes execution to branch out of the normal sequence. The control structure commands are immediate commands which compile the address literals and resolve the branch addresses.

One should note that BEGIN and THEN do not compile any token. They set up or resolve control structures in compound commands. IF, ELSE, WHILE, UNTIL, and AGAIN do compile address literals with branching tokens.

I use two characters a and A to denote two types of addresses on the parameter stack. a points to a location to where a branch commands would jump to. A points to a location where a new address will be stored when the address is resolved.

BEGIN	Start a loop structure. It pushes an address a onto the parameter stack. a points to the top of the dictionary where new tokens will be compiled. It begins an infinite loop or an indefinite loop.
FOR	Compile a >R token and pushes the address of the next token a on the parameter stack. It starts a FOR-NEXT loop.
NEXT	Compile a DONXT token with a target address a on the top of the parameter stack. It resolves a FOR NEXT loop.
UNTIL	Compile a QBRAN token with a target address a on the top of the parameter stack. It resolves a BEGIN-UNTIL loop.
AGAIN	Compile a BRAN token with a target address a on the top of the parameter stack. It resolves a BEGIN-AGAIN loop.
IF	Compile a QBRAN address literal and pushes its address, a, is left on the parameter stack. It starts a IF-ELSE-THEN or a IF-THEN branch structure.
AHEAD	Compile a BRAN address literal and pushes its address, a, is left on the parameter stack. It starts a AHEAD-THEN branch structure.
REPEAT	Compile a BRAN token with a target address a on the top of the parameter stack. It resolves a BEGIN-WHILE-REPEAT loop.
THEN	Resolve the address in a branch token whose address is a on the top of the parameter stack. It resolves a IF-ELSE-TEHN or IF-THEN branch structure.
AFT	Compile a BRAN literal and leaves its address as A, It also replaces the address a left by FOR with the address a1 of the next token. A will be used by THEN to resolve the AFT-THEN branch

	structure, and a1 will be used by NEXT to resolve the loop structure.
ELSE	Compile a BRAN token, and use the address of the next token to resolve the address field of QBRAN token in a, as left by IF. It also replaces a with A, the address of its address field for THEN to resolve. ELSE starts the false clause in the IF-ELSE-THEN branch structure.
WHILE	Compile a QBRAN token and leave its address, A, on the stack. Address a left by BEGIN is swapped to the top of the parameter stack. WHILE is used to start the true clause in the BEGIN-WHILE-REPEAT loop.

```
;; Structures

;    FOR        ( -- a )
;        Start a FOR-NEXT loop structure in a colon definition.
         .word  COMMA-2
         .byte  IMEDD+3,"FOR"
FOR
         $NEST
         .word  COMPI,TOR,BEGIN,EXIT


;    BEGIN      ( -- a )
;        Start an infinite or indefinite loop structure.
         .word  FOR-4
         .byte  IMEDD+5,"BEGIN"
BEGIN
         $NEST
         .word  CP,AT,EXIT


;    NEXT       ( a -- )
;        Terminate a FOR-NEXT loop structure.
         .word  BEGIN-6
         .byte  IMEDD+4,"NEXT",0
NEXT
         $NEST
         .word  COMPI,DONXT,COMMA,EXIT
```

```
;    UNTIL    ( a -- )
;        Terminate a BEGIN-UNTIL indefinite loop structure.
         .word  NEXT-6
         .byte  IMEDD+5,"UNTIL"
UNTIL
         $NEST
         .word  COMPI,QBRAN,COMMA,EXIT

;    AGAIN    ( a -- )
;        Terminate a BEGIN-AGAIN infinite loop structure.
         .word  UNTIL-6
         .byte  IMEDD+5,"AGAIN"
AGAIN
         $NEST
         .word  COMPI,BRAN,COMMA,EXIT

;    IF ( -- A )
;        Begin a conditional branch structure.
         .word  AGAIN-6
         .byte  IMEDD+2,"IF",0
IFF
         $NEST
         .word  COMPI,QBRAN,BEGIN
         .word  DOLIT,2,IALLOT,EXIT

;    AHEAD    ( -- A )
;        Compile a forward branch instruction.
;        .word  IFF-4
;        .byte  IMEDD+5,"AHEAD"
AHEAD
         $NEST
         .word  COMPI,BRAN,BEGIN
         .word  DOLIT,2,IALLOT,EXIT

;    REPEAT    ( A a -- )
;        Terminate a BEGIN-WHILE-REPEAT indefinite loop.
         .word  IFF-4
         .byte  IMEDD+6,"REPEAT",0
REPEA
```

```
        $NEST
        .word  AGAIN,BEGIN,SWAP,ISTORE,EXIT


;   THEN      ( A -- )
;       Terminate a conditional branch structure.
        .word  REPEA-8
        .byte  IMEDD+4,"THEN",0
THENN
        $NEST
        .word  BEGIN,SWAP,ISTORE,EXIT


;   AFT       ( a -- a A )
;       Jump to THEN in a FOR-AFT-THEN-NEXT loop the first time
through.
        .word  THENN-6
        .byte  IMEDD+3,"AFT"
AFT
        $NEST
        .word  DROP,AHEAD,BEGIN,SWAP,EXIT


;   ELSE      ( A -- A )
;       Start the false clause in an IF-ELSE-THEN structure.
        .word  AFT-4
        .byte  IMEDD+4,"ELSE",0
ELSEE
        $NEST
        .word  AHEAD,SWAP,THENN,EXIT


;   WHILE     ( a -- A a )
;       Conditional branch out of a BEGIN-WHILE-REPEAT loop.
        .word  ELSEE-6
        .byte  IMEDD+5,"WHILE"
WHILE
        $NEST
        .word  IFF,SWAP,EXIT


;   ABORT"    ( -- ; <string> )
;       Conditional abort with an error message.
        .word  WHILE-6
```

```
        .byte   IMEDD+6,"ABORT""",0
ABRTQ
        $NEST
        .word   COMPI,ABORQ,STRCQ,EXIT

;    $" ( -- ; <string> )
;        Compile an inline string literal.
        .word   ABRTQ-8
        .byte   IMEDD+2,"$""",0
STRQ
        $NEST
        .word   COMPI,STRQP,STRCQ,EXIT

;    ." ( -- ; <string> )
;        Compile an inline string literal to be typed out at run
time.
        .word   STRQ-4
        .byte   IMEDD+2,".""",0
DOTQ
        $NEST
        .word   COMPI,DOTQP,STRCQ,EXIT
```

Command Header

We had seen how tokens and structures are compiled into the code field of a compound command in the dictionary. To build a new command, we have to build its header first. A header consists of a link field and a name field. Here are the commands to build the header.

?UNIQUE	Display a warning message to show that the name of a new command already exists in the dictionary. Forth does not prevent your reusing the same name for different commands. However, giving the same name to different commands often causes problems in a software project. It is to be avoided if possible and ?UNIQUE reminds you of it.
$,n	Build a new header with a name string at RAM address na. It first build a link field with an address pointing to the name field of the prior command, and then copies the string at na to build a name

	field. The top of dictionary is now the code field of the new command, and tokens can be compiled.

```
;; Colon compiler

;    ?UNIQUE   ( a -- a )
;        Display a warning message if the word already exists.
;        .word DOTQ-4
;        .byte 7,"?UNIQUE"
UNIQU
        $NEST
        .word DUPP,NAMEQ     ;?name exists
        .word QBRAN,UNIQ1    ;redefinitions are OK
        .word DOTQP
        .byte 7," reDef "    ;but warn the user
        .word OVER,COUNT,TYPEE    ;just in case its not planned
UNIQ1:
        .word DROP,EXIT

;    $,n       ( na -- )
;        Build a new dictionary name using the string at na.
;        .word UNIQU-8
;        .byte 3,"$,n"
SNAME
        $NEST
        .word DUPP,CAT       ;?null input
        .word QBRAN,SNAM1
        .word UNIQU ;?redefinition
        .word LAST,AT,COMMA ;save na for vocabulary link
        .word CP,AT,LAST,STORE
        .word STRCQ1,EXIT    ;fill name field
SNAM1
        .word STRQP
        .byte 5," name"      ;null input
        .word ERROR
```

Colon Command Compiler

The command compiler is the most powerful feature of Forth. It compiles s new command which replaces a list of existing commands, and thus extend the Forth language by a small step. As Confucius said: "A journey of one thousand miles starts at the first step." These small steps build up entire applications. Keeping these steps small, they can be tested and debugged thoroughly. Replacing a list of tokens with one new token also elevates your application language to a higher level, from where you can see your forest clearer and farther, above the tree tops you had just scaled.

As I showed in the last section, command compiler compiles a new Forth command in the following form:

```
:  <new_command>  <name1>  <name2>  <name3>  ...  <nameN>  ;
```

Here we are at the peak of the 430eForth v4.3 system, and we have almost completed our tour.

$COMPILE	Compile one new token to the token list on the top of the dictionary. It takes a string address a on the top of the parameter stack, search dictionary for a matching command, and adds its execution address to the token list. If the string is not a valid command, it is converted to a number, and a integer literal added to the token list. If the string is not a number, abort the compilation process and return to the text interpreter loop QUIT. If the string is the name of an immediate command, this command is not compiled, but executed immediately. Immediate commands are tools used by the compiler to build structures in compound commands.
OVERT	Link a new command to the dictionary and thus makes it available for dictionary searches. When a new header is build, its name field address is stored in user variable LAST, and it is not yet linked to the dictionary which starts at CONTEXT. OVERT copies the name field address in LAST to CONTEXT and links the new command to the dictionary. It is used to protect the dictionary so that new commands not compiled successfully will not be linked incorrectly into the dictionary.
;	Terminate a new compound command. It compiles an EXIT token to terminate the new token list. It then links this new

	command to the dictionary, and then returns to the text interpreter by storing the code field address of $INTERPRET into user variable 'EVAL.
]	Turn the text interpreter to command compiler by storing the execution address of $COMPILE into user variable 'EVAL.
:	Create a new header and start a new compound command. It takes the following string in the input stream to be the name of the new command. The dictionary is ready to accept a token list.] turns the text interpreter into compiler, which will compile the following name strings to build a new compound command. The new compound command is terminated by ;.

```
;    $COMPILE  ( a -- )
;        Compile next word to code dictionary as a token or literal.
;        .word  UNIQU-8
;        .byte  8,"$COMPILE",0
SCOMP
        $NEST
        .word  NAMEQ,QDUP     ;?defined
        .word  QBRAN,SCOM2
        .word  AT,DOLIT,IMEDD,ANDD ;?immediate
        .word  QBRAN,SCOM1
        .word  EXECU,EXIT     ;its immediate, execute
SCOM1: .word  COMMA,EXIT     ;its not immediate, compile
SCOM2: .word  NUMBQ ;try to convert to number
        .word  QBRAN,SCOM3
        .word  LITER,EXIT     ;compile number as integer
SCOM3: .word  ERROR  ;error


;    OVERT     ( -- )
;        Link a new word into the current vocabulary.
;        .word  SCOMP-10
;        .byte  5,"OVERT"
OVERT
        $NEST
        .word  LAST,AT,CNTXT,STORE,EXIT
```

```
;     ;    ( -- )
;          Terminate a colon definition.
           .word  DOTQ-4
           .byte  IMEDD+COMPO+1,";"
SEMIS
           $NEST
           .word  COMPI,EXIT,LBRAC,OVERT,EXIT


;     ]    ( -- )
;          Start compiling the words in the input stream.
           .word  SEMIS-2
           .byte  1,"]"
RBRAC
           $NEST
           .word  DOLIT,SCOMP,TEVAL,STORE,EXIT


;     :    ( -- ; <string> )
;          Start a new colon definition using next word as its name.
           .word  RBRAC-2
           .byte  1,":"
COLON
           $NEST
           .word  TOKEN,SNAME,DOLIT,DOLST
           .word  CALLC,RBRAC,EXIT
```

Defining Commands

Defining commands are molds which can be used to create classes of commands which share the same run time execution behavior. In 430eForth, we have these defining commands: : , CREATE, CONSTANT and VARIABLE.

HEADER	Create a header of a constant command in flash memory. It assembles a call #DOCON machine instruction. This header is shared by CREATE, CONSTANT and VARIABLE. When DOCON is executed, it pushes the contents of the next cell on the parameter stack. This is the value of a constant, or a RAM pointer for a variable, or pointer to an array

	in RAM. Variables cannot be stored in flash memory, and they must be allocated spaces in RAM memory.
CREATE	Create a new data array in RAM memory without allocating memory. When a command created by CREATE is executed, it pushes a RAM address on the parameter stack. Memory space of an actual array is allocated using ALLOT command.
CONSTANT	Create a new command with a call #DOCON instruction followed by the constant value. When a constant command is executed, it pushes the constant value on the parameter stack.
VARIABLE	Create a new command with a call #DOCON instruction followed by a pointer to RAM memory and allocate 2 bytes of space in RAM memory. When a variable commands is executed, it pushes this RAM address on the parameter stack.
IMMEDIATE (Not implemented)	Set the immediate lexicon bit in the name field of the new command. When the compiler encounters a command with this bit set, it will not compile this command into the token list under construction, but execute it immediately. This bit allows immediate commands to build special structures in compound commands, and to deal with special conditions while compiling. However, this command does not work with commands compiled in flash memory, which does not allow cleared bit to be set again. 430eForth v4.3 thus does not allow you to define an immediate command. It is not a great lost because very few applications actually require this very special Forth feature.

```
;; Defining words

;    HEADER    ( -- ; <string> )
;       Compile a new array entry without allocating code space.
;       .word   DOCON-6
;       .byte   6,"HEADER",0
```

```
HEADER
        $NEST
        .word  TOKEN,SNAME,OVERT
        .word  DOLIT,DOCON,CALLC,EXIT

;   CREATE    ( -- ; <string> )
;       Compile a new array entry without allocating code space.
        .word  COLON-2
        .byte  6,"CREATE",0
CREAT
        $NEST
        .word  HEADER,DP,AT,COMMA,EXIT

;   CONSTANT ( n -- ; <string> )
;       Compile a new constant.
        .word  CREAT-8
        .byte  8,"CONSTANT",0
CONST
        $NEST
        .word  HEADER,COMMA,EXIT

;   VARIABLE  ( -- ; <string> )
;       Compile a new variable initialized to 0.
        .word  CONST-10
        .byte  8,"VARIABLE",0
VARIA
        $NEST
        .word  CREAT,DOLIT,2,ALLOT,EXIT
```

4.5 Tools

430eForth is a very small system and only a very small set of tool commands are provided. Nevertheless, this set of tool commands is powerful enough to help you debug new commands you add to the system. They are also very interesting programming examples on how to use the commands in Forth to build applications.

Generally, the tool commands present information stored in different parts of the CPU in appropriate formats to let you inspect the results as you executes commands in the

Forth system and commands you defined yourself. The tool commands include names searching, memory dump, stack dump, and dictionary dump.

'	Search the dictionary for the following string. If the string is the name of a valid command, return its token or execution address. If the string is not a valid name, display a ? mark.

```
;; Tools

;      '   ( -- ca )
;        Search context vocabularies for the next word in input
stream.
        .word  VARIA-10
        .byte  1,"'"
TICK
        $NEST
        .word  TOKEN,NAMEQ   ;?defined
        .word  QBRAN,TICK1
        .word  EXIT    ;yes, push code address
TICK1:
        .word  ERROR  ;no, error
```

Memory Dump

One important discipline in Forth programming is to learn how to use the parameter stack correctly, and effectively. All commands must consume their input parameters on the stack and leave only their intended results on the stack. Sloppy usage of the parameter stack is often the cause of bugs which are very difficult to detect later, as unexpected items left on the stack could result in unpredictable behavior. .S should be used liberally during programming and debugging to ensure that the correct parameters are consumed or left on the parameter stack.

DUMP allows you inspect memory at any address, RAM, flash, and I/O registers. You can inspect both data and code. You can use it to monitor and control I/O devices. It makes you feel that you are the master of your computer.

It is nice to visualize memory which is organized in fixed length pages. 128 bytes are a good size to view on a terminal screen. DUMP is very useful to inspect one page of memory conveniently. Here are some examples of memory dumps:

```
0 DUMP           CPU registers and special function registers
HEX 80 DUMP      The rest of IO registers
C000 DUMP        Reset area of code memory
1000 DUMP        Information D memory for user variable
```

DUMP	Display 128 bytes of data starting at memory address b to the terminal. It dumps 16 bytes to a line. A line begins with the address of the first byte, followed by 16 bytes shown in hex, 3 columns per bytes. At the end of a line are the 16 bytes shown in ASCII characters. Non-printable characters are replaced by underscores (ASCII 95). DUMP command in most Forth system takes an address and a length as parameters to dump a memory array. I am getting tired to type the length of array.

```
;    DUMP      ( a u -- )
;        Dump u bytes from a, in a formatted manner.
         .word  TICK-2
         .byte  4,"DUMP",0
DUMP
         $NEST
         .word  DOLIT,7,TOR   ;start count down loop
DUMP1:
         .word  CR,DUPP,DOLIT,5,UDOTR
         .word  DOLIT,15,TOR
DUMP2:
         .word  COUNT,DOLIT,3,UDOTR
         .word  DONXT,DUMP2   ;loop till done
         .word  SPACE,DUPP,DOLIT,16,SUBB
         .word  DOLIT,16,TYPEE      ;display printable characters
         .word  DONXT,DUMP1   ;loop till done
         .word  DROP,EXIT
```

Parameter Stack Dump

One important discipline in learning Forth is to learn how to use the parameter stack correctly and effectively. All commands must consume their input parameters on the stack and leave only their intended results on the stack. Sloppy usage of the parameter stack is often the cause of bugs which are very difficult to detect later, as unexpected items left on the stack could result in unpredictable behavior. .S should be used liberally during programming and debugging to ensure that the correct parameters are consumed and left on the parameter stack.

The parameter stack is the center for arithmetic and logic operations. It is where commands receive their parameters and also where they left their results. In debugging a new command which may use stack items and leave items on the stack, the best was to debug it is to inspect the parameter stack, before and after its execution. To inspect the parameter stack non-destructively, use the command .S.

.S	Display the contents of the parameter stack in the free format. The bottom of the stack is aligned to the left margin. The top item is shown towards the right and followed by the characters <top .S does not change the parameter stack so it can be used to inspect the parameter stack non-destructively at any time.

```
;       .S ( ... -- ... )
;          Display the contents of the data stack.
           .word  DUMP-6
           .byte  2,".S",0
DOTS
           $NEST
           .word  CR,DEPTH       ;stack depth
           .word  TOR     ;start count down loop
           .word  BRAN,DOTS2     ;skip first pass
DOTS1:
           .word  RAT,PICK,DOT ;index stack, display contents
DOTS2:
           .word  DONXT,DOTS1   ;loop till done
           .word  DOTQP
           .byte  4," <sp",0
           .word  EXIT
```

Dictionary Dump

The dictionary contains all command records defined in the system, ready for execution and compilation. WORDS command allows you to examine the dictionary and to look for the correct names of commands in case you are not sure of their spellings. WORDS follows the dictionary link in the user variable CONTEXT and displays the names of all commands in the dictionary, in the reversed order. The dictionary links can be traced easily because the link field in the header of a command points to the name field of the previous command, and the link field is two bytes below the corresponding name field.

>NAME	Return a code field address, xt, of a command from its name field address, na. If xt is not a valid code field address, return 0. It follows the linked list of the dictionary, and from every name field address we can get a corresponding code field address. If this address is not the same as xt, we go to the name field of the next command. If xt is a valid code field address, we surely will find it. If the entire dictionary is searched and xt is not found, it is not a valid code field address, or it does not have a name field.
.ID	Display the name of a command, given the name field address of this command. It replaces non-printable characters in a name by under-scores.
WORDS	Display all the names in the dictionary. The order of words is reversed from the compiled order. The last defined command is shown first.

```
;    >NAME      ( ca -- na | F )
;        Convert code address to a name address.
;        .word DOTS-4
;        .byte 5,">NAME"
TNAME
         $NEST
         .word TOR,CNTXT,AT  ;vocabulary link
TNAM1:
         .word DUPP,QBRAN,TNAM2
         .word DUPP,NAMET,RAT,XORR  ;compare
         .word QBRAN,TNAM2
```

```
        .word  CELLM  ;continue with next word
        .word  AT,BRAN,TNAM1
TNAM2:
        .word  RFROM,DROP,EXIT


;    .ID         ( na -- )
;       Display the name at address.
;       .word  TNAME-6
;       .byte  3,".ID"
DOTID
        $NEST
        .word  COUNT,DOLIT,01FH,ANDD        ;mask lexicon bits
        .word  TYPEE,EXIT


;    WORDS      ( -- )
;       Display the names in the context vocabulary.
        .word  DOTS-4
        .byte  5,"WORDS"
WORDS
        $NEST
        .word  CR,CNTXT,AT   ;only in context
WORS1:
        .word  QDUP   ;?at end of list
        .word  QBRAN,WORS2
        .word  DUPP,SPACE,DOTID      ;display a name
        .word  CELLM,AT,BRAN,WORS1
WORS2:
        .word  EXIT
```

Forth Cold Start

The startup routine main is located at the very beginning of the flash main memory, at location C000H. It initializes the return stack pointer in the sp register, and the parameter stack pointer in stack and tos register. It thus completes hardware initialization, and then jumps to COLD command which initializes the 430eForth Forth Virtual Machine, by copying the user variables from flash information memory Segment D (at 1000H) to RAM memory starting at 200H, and starts running an application. The default application in 430eForth is HI, which simply sends out a sign-on message and falls into the text interpreter QUIT. The address of HI is stored in memory location named 'BOOT at 200H. This address can be changed to point to your application command. To build a turnkey system, the user variables must be saved in Segment D so that when the application boots up, it has all the properly initialized user variables.

Because all the user variables in 430eForth are initialized from a data array in the information flash memory, 430eForth is eminently ROMable and suitable for embedded applications in MSP430G2553. Before falling into the text interpreter loop QUIT, COLD command executes a boot routine whose code address is stored in user variable 'BOOT.

APP! stores an execution address of your application in 'BOOT and saves all user variables in flash memory Segment D, and thus builds a turnkey system for you. Your application command will run on power-up and on reset. Initially 'BOOT contains the code field address of HI.

HI	The default start-up routine in 430eForth. It displays a sign-on message.
APP!	Store the execution address of your application command on top of parameter stack into user variable 'BOOT, erase the flash Information D memory, and copy all user variables from RAM memory address $200-215 to Information D memory at $1000. This is how you customize your Forth system. When you reset LaunchPad, it starts executing your own application.
COLD	A high level compound command executed upon power-up, called from the initial main routine. Its initializes the user variables, executes the boot-up routine vectored through 'BOOT, and then falls into the text interpreter loop QUIT.

```
;; Cold boot

;    HI ( -- )
;        Display the sign-on message of eForth.
         .word  WORDS-6
         .byte  2,"HI",0
HI
         $NEST
         .word  CR,DOTQP
```

```
        .byte   14,"430eForth v4.3",0         ;model
        .word   CR,EXIT


;    APP!      ( a -- )        Turnkey
;       HEX : APP! 200 ! 1000 ERASE 200 1000 20 WRITE ;
        .word   HI-4
        .byte   4,"APP!",0
APPST
        $NEST
        .word   TBOOT,STORE,DOLIT,0x1000,IERASE
        .word   TBOOT,DOLIT,0x1000,DOLIT,0x20
        .word   WRITE,EXIT


;    COLD      ( -- )
;       The hilevel cold start sequence.
        .word   APPST-6
        .byte   4,"COLD",0
COLD
        $NEST
        .word   STOIO
        .word   DOLIT,UZERO,DOLIT,UPP
        .word   DOLIT,ULAST-UZERO,CMOVE       ;initialize user area
        .word   TBOOT,ATEXE   ;application boot
        .word   QUIT    ;start interpretation


CTOP
```

Initial User Variables

The first 24 bytes starting at location $200 are used by user variables, as shown in the following list:

Variable	Address	Function
'BOOT	200H	Execution vector to start application command.
BASE	202H	Radix base for numeric conversion.
tmp	204H	Scratch pad.

HLD	206H	Pointer to a buffer holding next digit for numeric conversion.
>IN	208H	Input buffer character pointer used by text interpreter.
#TIB	20AH	Number of characters in input buffer.
'EVAL	20CH	Execution vector switching between $INTERPRET and $COMPILE.
CONTEXT	210H	Vocabulary array pointing to last name fields of dictionary.
CP	212H	Pointer to top of dictionary, the first available flash memory location to compile new command
DP	214H	Pointer to the first available RAM memory location.
LAST	216H	Pointer to name field of last command in dictionary.

The initial values of user variable are stored in the information flash memory Segment D at location 1000H. The assembly commands .sect ".infoD" direct the linker to store these initial values there so that the COLD routine can initializes the user variables properly after boot-up.

The assembly commands .sect ".reset" direct the linker to store the address of main in the reset vector at 0FFFEH, so that MSP430G2553 jumps to main on boot-up.

```
;;;;;;;;;;;;;;;;;;;;;;;;;;;;;;;;;;;;;;;;;;;;;;;;;;;;;;;;;;

;;;;
; COLD start moves the following to user variables.

        .sect  ".infoD"
UZERO:
        .word  HI       ;200H, boot routine
        .word  BASEE    ;202H, BASE
        .word  0        ;204H, tmp
        .word  0        ;206H, >IN
        .word  0        ;208H, #TIB
        .word  0        ;20AH, HLD
```

```
        .word   INTER   ;20CH, 'EVAL
        .word   COLD-6 ;20EH, CONTEXT pointer
        .word   CTOP+8 ;210H, CP; pass ISR
        .word   DPP     ;220H, DP
        .word   COLD-6 ;214H, LAST
ULAST:

;================================================
        .sect   ".reset"    ; MSP430 RESET Vector
        .short  main ;
        .end
;================================================
```

That's All! Folks!

Conclusions

Here we are. You've seen the following picture, that of a MSP430G2 LaunchPad Kit. What I had talked about was this 20-pin DIP chip in the middle of the Kit, the MSP430G2553 microcontroller. It looks plain and ordinary, just another 20-pin DIP chip. The silicon chip inside is even smaller, about 4 mm².

However, its processing power is equivalent to the ENIAC, the first electronic computer built in 1946. In 70 years, with equivalent capability, the computer size, costs, and power consumption are all reduced by a factor of 10,000,000. This is Zen in computer hardware. So much computing power is consolidated in a very small package, and made available to everybody who has an interest in using it. With a microcontroller smaller than a finger nail, it is up to us firmware engineers to make it do useful work, for the benefits of humanity.

The reduction in size, costs, and power in computer hardware is not matched by the complexity in software and in software engineering. The size and complexity in operating systems and programming tools chains grows as computers are getting bigger and bigger. As one of Parkinson's Laws states that the software grows to fill all available memory space. In 1957, FORTRAN was developed to ease programming efforts, and it became hugely successful.

However, FORTRAN was the wrong programming language for computers in general. It gets computers to do algebra instead of arithmetic, which computers do naturally, as all computers have ALU, Arithmetic/Logic Unit, in them. Most high level programming languages followed FORTRAN closely, including C, using algebraic equations as the elementary construct in programs. Since algebra is not natural to computers, algebraic equations have to be translated or compiled into arithmetic expressions that computers can work on.

As far as mathematics is concerned, Forth is an arithmetic and logic language, and it does not need complicated compilers to translate algebraic equations. All arithmetic and logic operations are done in a left to right sequence. No artificial parentheses and rules of precedence are necessary. Actually, the left to right execution sequence applies equally well to almost all other types of operations. Forth is thus closer to a natural language than all other languages, programming languages and linguistic languages, which always require syntax rules and grammatical constructs to clarify the intentions of the speaker.

The left to right interpretation of command lists, and the capability to name a list to become a new command is the natural way we human thinks, communicates, and to develop intelligence. I capture this intelligence in 430eForth on a LaunchPad. In 4136 bytes, you have a programming language, an interactive operating system, and all the debugging tools to develop applications on LaunchPad Kit, for LaunchPad Kit.

The complete source code of 430eForth.asm is only 40 Kbytes long. It is an organic system, which can grow to accommodate any application that MSP430G2553 microcontroller can host. It allows you to read all its CPU and I/O registers, and all its data and program memories. It also allows you to change the I/O registers and memories, and to add new commands to the flash memory. By adding new commands, you can extend the 430eForth system and build a new system which will do what you want it to do.

In 430eForth v4.3, I try to reduce the Forth language to its bare minimum, so that you can have a small, fast and easy to use Forth system to learn this programming language quickly, and to use it to do useful work. I like you to have a Zen system in software to match the Zen system in the hardware of LaunchPad. As you use it to build firmware engineering projects, you will spend lots of time meditate on the hardware and software components. If you do it long enough, I am sure you will gain an understanding that LaunchPad is a natural extension of yourself. Whatever you think, you can transfer it to LaunchPad and have it done your wishes. This is enlightenment and Zen.

I love to tell you another story about Zen. This was how the Sixth Patriarch Huineng got the garment and the bowl, symbols of enlightenment, from the Fifth Patriarch Hungjen.

Huineng, the Sixth Patriarch, was a genius. He couldn't read because he was borne poor and gathered wood for a living, but he could explain the Sutras when people read them to him. He went to learn from the Fifth Patriarch Hungjen, and Hungjen sent him instead to labor in the kitchen. As Hungjen got old and wanted to pass on his garment and his bowl, he asked his students to write poems to show him their understanding of the enlightenment. His best student Shenhsiu wrote the following poem:

身是菩提樹，My body is the bodhi tree,
心如明鏡臺。And my mind a mirror bright.
時時勤拂拭，Carefully I wipe them hour by hour,
勿使惹塵埃。And let no dust alight.

Hearing this poem, Huineng asked a scholar to write down his own poem, because he couldn't write himself:

菩提本無樹，There is no bodhi tree,
明鏡亦非臺。Nor stand of a mirror bright.
本來無一物，Since all is void,
何處惹塵埃。Where can the dust alight?

When Hungjen saw this poem, he passed the garment and the bowl to Huineng and told Huineng: "You are the one Boddhidharma prophesied. Zen will flourish in China through you. Take the garment and the bowl to be the Sixth Patriarch, but do not pass them on any more." Hungjen was in such a hurry to pass things to Huineng that he didn't even shave Huineng's hair (to admit him to Buddhist order), as Huineng was still a layman.

Years later, Huineng formed the Southern Sudden School of Zen, and Shenhsiu formed the Northern Gradual School of Zen. Huineng advocated that enlightenment and Zen was achieved suddenly with special inspiration. Shenhsiu advocated that enlightenment and Zen could be achieved gradually, only by longtime meditation, reading and studying.

Applying their thoughts to computers, Shenhsiu's view was realistic and practical. Computers are complicated, and software is complicated, because people made them complicated. You have to study hard to get through the maze. Huineng's view was more romantic and drastic. Computers do not have to be complicated. Software does not have to be complicated.

If you have the understanding, computers can be made simple, and software can be made simple. You have to get to the essence of them and eliminate all the parts which are not essential. Once you get the core of things working, you can extend it in any direction and make it as complicated as you wish. But, you still have to maintain control. If you lose control, computers can be your worst enemies. If you can maintain control, computers are your best friends.

The essence of computers does not come by itself. You need to know it, by diligent reading, studying, and experimentations. A period of confusion, bewilderment, and puzzlement is unavoidable. You are in the Northern Gradual School. When your knowledge and understanding build up gradually, at one point, all the pieces of the big puzzle suddenly fall into place. When the computer finally understands you, or better, when you finally understand your computer, enlightenment strikes, and you find yourself in the Southern Sudden School, winning a trophy of Zen.

When you hold a LaunchPad Kit in your hand, you know that the only important thing on it is the 20-pin DIP MSP430G2553 chip. Can things get simpler? Then, you are confronted with this huge manual *MSP430x2x22 User's Guide.* It takes the 658 pages to explain this small chip.

Like all other microcontrollers and for that matter, all other computers, MSP430G2553 chip was designed by groups of engineers who did not understand microcontrollers, and how they were to be used. They managed to squeeze lots of devices and features into a small chip. They then threw the chip over a wall to the software engineers, who built assemblers, compilers and debugging tools.

They dumped this huge tool chain in your lap, and hope that you can build something useful out of the whole mess. In 430eForth, I am telling these hardware and software engineers how to design a useful and easy to use microcontroller, in terms of a Forth Virtual Machine. They should implement as many primitive commands as machine instructions. If they missed any, it was not a problem. I can synthesize any missing machine instruction in compound commands.

Any command set I can give you will not be enough, because I cannot anticipate your needs and your application. If I miss any, it is not a problem. Because I am also giving you the tools to synthesize any command that you need. You can design the exact command set to solve your problem.

Modern computers with ever increasing circuitry, speed and memory, host ever bigger and more complicated software. They are designed to enslave people. You are not taught how hardware and software work. You are taught to push certain buttons, and you are taught to type certain keys. Then, you get employed to push buttons and to type keys to work as slaves until you die. Computers, programming languages, and operating systems are made complicated to enslave you.

Computers are not complicated beyond comprehension. Programming languages and operating systems do not have to be complicated. They are all within your grasp if you are determined to get to the bottom of them. LaunchPad is a good example. It is a complicated chip. However, here is a magic key which can unlock the microcontroller, and make it plain and approachable. The text interpreter in 430eForth makes MSP430G2553 chip your friend. You can talk to it, you can ask it questions, and you can ask it to do things. You may even fall in love with it.

As a lifelong teacher, I really enjoy microcontrollers as students. Most students generally did not remember what you taught them in classes, after the final examination. Then, you would appreciate a student who actually remembers something you taught him. Microcontrollers are my best students, because they have perfect memory, and they remembered everything I taught them, right or wrong.

What else could you ask of a student? You taught them wrong things, because you hadn't learnt the right thing yet. But, no matter. In them, you will find what you did wrong and correct your mistakes. Until one day, you give it a command, and it does the job perfectly. This is Zen, and this is what I hope you will get.

Let's get back to the first Zen story about Śākyamuni Buddha and his flower. He raised a flower, and Mahākāśyapa smiled. Here, I have this LaunchPad in my hand. Do I see a smile?

Appendix 430eForth Commands

Stack Comments:

Stack inputs and outputs are shown in the form: (input1 input2 ... -- output1 output2 ...)

Stack Abbreviations of Number Types

flag	Boolean flag, either 0 or –1
char	ASCII character or a byte
n	16 bit number
addr	16 bit address
d	32 bit number

Stack Manipulation Commands

?DUP	(n -- n n | 0)	Duplicate top of stack if it is not 0.
DUP	(n – n n)	Duplicate top of stack.
DROP	(n --)	Discard top of stack.
SWAP	(n1 n2 -- n2 n1)	Exchange top two stack items.
OVER	(n1 n2 -- n1 n2 n1)	Make copy of second item on stack.
ROT	(n1 n2 n3 -- n2 n3 n1)	Rotate third item to top.
PICK	(n -- n1)	Zero based, duplicate nth item to top. (e.g. 0 PICK is DUP).
>R	(n --)	Move top item to return stack for temporary storage.
R>	(-- n)	Retrieve top item from return stack.
R@	(-- n)	Copy top of return stack onto stack.
2DUP	(d -- d d)	Duplicate double number on top of stack.
2DROP	(d1 d2 --)	Discard two double numbers on top of stack
DEPTH	(-- n)	Count number of items on stack.

Arithmetic Commands

+	(n1 n2 -- n3)	Add n1 and n2.
–	(n1 n2 -- n3)	Subtract n2 from n1 (n1–n2=n3).
*	(n1 n2 -- n3)	Multiply. n3=n1*n2
/	(n1 n2 -- n3)	Division, signed (n3= n1/n2).
2*	(n -- n*2)	Logic left shift.

209

2/	(n -- n/2)	Logic right shift.
UM+	(n1 n2 -- nd)	Unsigned addition, double precision result.
UM*	(n1 n2 -- nd)	Unsigned multiply, double precision result.
M*	(n n -- d)	Signed multiply. Return double product.
UM/MOD	(nd n1 -- mod quot)	Unsigned division with double precision dividend.
M/MOD	(d n -- mod quot)	Signed floored divide of double by single. Return mod and quotient.
MOD	(n1 n2 -- mod)	Modulus, signed (remainder of n1/n2).
/MOD	(n1 n2 -- mod quot)	Division with both remainder and quotient.
*/MOD	(n1 n2 n3 -- n4 n5)	Multiply and then divide (n1*n2/n3)
*/	(n1 n2 n3 -- n4)	Like */MOD, but with quotient only.
ABS	(n1 -- n2)	If n1 is negative, n2 is its two's complement.
NEGATE	(n1 -- n2)	Two's complement.
MAX	(n1 n2 -- n3)	n3 is the larger of n1 and n2.
MIN	(n1 n2 -- n3)	n3 is the smaller of n1 and n2.
DNEGATE	(d1 -- d2)	Negate double number. Two's complement.
D+	(d1 d2 -- d3)	Add double numbers.

Logic and Comparison Commands

AND	(n1 n2 -- n3)	Logical bit-wise AND.
OR	(n1 n2 -- n3)	Logical bit-wise OR.
XOR	(n1 n2 -- n3)	Logical bit-wise exclusive OR.
NOT	(n1 -- n2)	Bit-wise one's complement.
0<	(n -- flag)	True if n is negative.
U<	(n1 n2 -- flag)	True if n1 less than n2. Unsigned compare.
<	(n1 n2 -- flag)	True if n1 less than n2.
=	(n1 n2 -- flag)	True if n1 equals n2.
>	(n1 n2 -- flag)	True if n1 greater than n2.

RAM Memory Commands

@	(addr -- n)	Replace addr by number at addr.
C@	(addr -- char)	Fetch least-significant byte only.
!	(n addr --)	Store n at addr.
C!	(char addr --)	Store least-significant byte only.
+!	(n addr --)	Add n to number at addr.
COUNT	(addr1 -- addr+1 char)	Move string count from memory onto stack.
ALLOT	(n --)	Add n bytes to the RAM pointer DP.
HERE	(-- addr)	Address of next available RAM memory location.
PAD	(-- addr)	Address of a scratch area of at least 64 bytes.
TIB	(-- addr)	Address of terminal input buffer.
CMOVE	(addr1 addr2 n --)	Move n bytes starting at memory addr1 to addr2.
FILL	(addr n char --)	Fill n bytes of memory at addr with char.

Flash Memory Commands

I!	(n addr --)	Store n at flash memory addr.
IALLOT	(n --)	Add n bytes to the flash memory pointer CP.
WRITE	(addr1 addr2 --)	Write 128 bytes from RAM memory addr1 to flash memory addr2.
ERASE	(addr --)	Erase an 128 byte page in flash memory at addr.

User Variables

'BOOT	(-- addr)	Contains address of application command to boot.
BASE	(-- addr)	Contains radix for number conversion
CP	(-- addr)	Contains first free address in flash memory
DP	(-- addr)	Contains first free address in RAM memory

Terminal Input-Output Commands

EMIT	(char --)	Display char.
KEY	(-- char)	Get an ASCII character from the keyboard.
?KEY	(-- char -1 | 0)	Return an ASCII character from the keyboard and a true flag. Return false flag if no character available.
.	(n --)	Display number n with a trailing blank.
U.	(n --)	Display an unsigned integer with a trailing blank.
.R	(n1 n2 --)	Display signed number n1 right justified in n2 character field.
U.R	(n1 n2 --)	Display unsigned number n1 right justified in n2 character field.
?	(addr --)	Display contents at memory addr.
<#	(--)	Start numeric output string conversion.
#	(n1 -- n2)	Convert next digit of number and add to output string
#S	(n --)	Convert all significant digits in n to output string.
HOLD	(char --)	Add char to output string.
SIGN	(n --)	If n is negative, add a minus sign to the output string.
#>	(xd -- addr n)	Terminate numeric string, leaving addr and count for TYPE.
CR	(--)	Display a new line.
SPACE	(--)	Display a space.
SPACES	(n --)	Display n spaces.
ACCEPT	(addr n --)	Accept n characters into buffer at addr.
CHAR	(-- char)	Parse next command and return its first character.
TYPE	(addr n --)	Display a string of n characters starting at address addr.
BL	(-- 32)	Return ASCII Blank character.
DECIMAL	(--)	Set number base to decimal.
HEX	(--)	Set number base to hexadecimal.

Compiler and Interpreter Commands

:<name>	(--)	Begin a colon definition of <name>.
;	(--)	Terminate execution of a colon definition.
CREATE <name>	(--)	Dictionary entry with no parameter field space reserved.
VARIABLE <name>	(--)	Defines a variable. At run-time, <name> leaves its address.
CONSTANT <name>	(n --)	Defines a constant. At run-time, n is left on the stack.
,	(n --)	Compile n to the dictionary in flash memory
[	(--)	Switch from compilation to interpretation.
]	(--)	Switch from interpretation to compilation.
WORD<text>	(char -- addr)	Get the char delimited string <text> from the input stream and leave as a counted string at addr.
TOKEN	(-- addr)	Parse next word from input stream and copy it to name buffer in RAM at addr.
(comment)	(--)	Ignore comment text.
\ comment	(--)	Ignore comment till end of line.
." <text>"	(--)	Compile <text> message. At run-time display text message.
.(<text>)	(--)	Display <text> from the input stream.
$" <text>"	(-- addr)	Compile <text> message. At run-time return its address.
ABORT" <text>"	(flag --)	Compile <test> message. At run-time display message and abort if flag is true. Otherwise, ignore message and continue.
COLD	(--)	Start eForth system.
QUIT	(--)	Return to interpret mode, clear data and return stacks.

QUERY	(--)	Accept input stream to terminal input buffer.
NUMBER?	(addr -- n -1 | addr 0)	Convert a number string to integer. Push a flag on tos.
EXECUTE	(addr --)	Execute command definition at addr.
@EXECUTE	(addr --)	Execute command definition whose execution address is in addr.
EXIT	(--)	Terminate execution of a colon definition.

Compiler Structure Commands

IF	(flag --)	If flag is zero, branches forward to ELSE or THEN.
ELSE	(--)	Branch forward to THEN.
THEN	(--)	Terminate a IF-ELSE-THEN structure.
FOR	(n --)	Setup loop with n as index. Repeat loop n+1 times.
NEXT	(--)	Decrement loop index by 1 and branch back to FOR. Terminate FOR-NEXT loop when index is negative.
AFT	(--)	Branch forward to THEN in a loop to skip the first round
BEGIN	(--)	Start an indefinite loop.
AGAIN	(--)	Branch backward to BEGIN.
UNTIL	(flag --)	Branch backward to BEGIN if flag is false. If flag is true, terminate BEGIN-UNTIL loop.
WHILE	(flag --)	If flag is false, branch forward to terminate BEGIN-WHILE-REPEAT loop. If flag is true, continue execution till REPEAT.
REPEAT	(--)	Resolve WHILE clause. Branch backward to BEGIN.

Utility Commands

' <name>	(-- addr)	Look up <name> in the dictionary. Return execution address.
DUMP	(addr --)	Dump 128 bytes of RAM memory starting from addr.
.S	(--)	Dump the parameter stack.
WORDS	(--)	Display all eForth commands
HI	(--)	Default application. Display sign-on message.
APP!	(addr --)	Build a turnkey system to execute an application at addr.

####

Dr. Chen-Hanson Ting

Introduction:

Retired chemist-turned-engineer

How long have you been interested in Forth: 32 years

Bio:

PhD in chemistry, University of Chicago, 1965.

Professor of chemistry in Taiwan until 1975.

Firmware engineer in Silicon Valley until retirement in 2000.

Still actively composing Forth Haikus.

Custodian of the eForth systems since 1990

Still maintaining eForth systems for
Arduino, MSP430, and various ARM microcontrollers.

Author of eP8, eP16, eP24, and eP32 microcontrollers in VHDL,
which were implemented on several FPGA chips.

Offete Enterprises, started in 1975, and is now formally closed.

However, Dr. Ting can still be contacted
through email chenhting@yahoo.com.tw

(source www.forth.org/whoswho.html#chting)

Exeter / UK – ExMark – Juergen Pintaske – October 2018